VOLUME ONE
ISSUE TWO
JULY 2004
HOME
CULTURES

AF479000

BERG

AIMS AND SCOPES

Home Cultures is an interdisciplinary journal dedicated to the critical understanding of the domestic sphere, its artefacts, spaces and relations, across timeframes and cultures. Whether as a concept or a physical place, "home" is a highly fluid and contested site of human existence that reflects and reifies identities and values. The Journal aims to promote a conversation about the domestic sphere across the many disciplines in which "home" forms a key unit of analysis. By generating a site for interdisciplinary discussion and comparative approaches, *Home Cultures* provides a vital and diverse forum for our general understanding of this vital sphere of human activity.

Towards this aim, the editors invite submissions from a broad range of scholars and practitioners, including: design practices, design history, social history, literary studies, architecture, gender studies, cultural/social history, anthropology, sociology, archaeology, urban planning, legal studies, contemporary art, geography, psychology, folklore, cultural studies, literary studies and art history.

Anyone wishing to submit an article, interview, book, film or exhibition review for possible publication in this journal should contact the editors at,

homecultures@ucl.ac.uk

Notes for contributors can be found at the back of the journal.

©2004 Berg. All rights reserved. No part of this publication may be reproduced or utilized in any form or by any means, electronic or mechanical, including photocopying and recording, or by any information storage or retrieval system, without permission in writing from the publisher.

ISSN: 1740-6315

SUBSCRIPTION INFORMATION

Three issues per volume.

One volume per annum.

2004: Volume 1

ONLINE
www.bergpublishers.com

BY MAIL
Berg Publishers
C/o Customer Services
Extenza-Turpin
Pegasus Drive
Stratton Business Park
Biggleswade
Bedfordshire SG18 8TQ
UK

BY FAX
+44 (0)1767 601640

BY TELEPHONE
+44 (0)1767 604800

INQUIRIES

Editorial: Kathryn Earle, Managing Editor, email: kearle@bergpublishers.com

Production: Ken Bruce, email: kbruce@bergpublishers.com

Advertising and subscriptions: Amelia La Fuente, email: ALafuente@bergpublishers.com

SUBSCRIPTION RATES

Institutions' subscription rate £125/US$195

Individuals' subscription rate £45/US$72*

*This price is available only to personal subscribers and must be prepaid by personal cheque or credit card

Free online subscription for print subscribers

Full colour images available online

Access your electronic subscription through www.ingenta.com or www.ingentaselect.com

REPRINTS FOR MAILING

Copies of individual articles may be obtained from the publishers at the appropriate fees.
Write to

Berg Publishers
1st Floor, Angel Court
81 St Clements Street
Oxford OX4 1AW
UK

EDITORS

Victor Buchli
University College London, UK

Alison Clarke
University of Applied Arts, Vienna, Austria

Dell Upton
University of Virginia, USA

ADVISORY BOARD

Judith Attfield, Winchester School of Art, University of Southampton, UK

Leora Auslander, University of Chicago, USA

Iain Borden, The Bartlett School of Architecture, University College London, UK

Peter Burke, University of Cambridge, UK

Sophie Chevalier, Université de Franche-Comté, France

Irene Cieraad, Delft University of Technology, Netherlands

Elizabeth Cromley, Northeastern University, USA

Inge Daniels, AHRB Centre for the Study of the Domestic Interior, UK

Prof. Sir Christopher Frayling, Rector of the Royal College of Art, UK

Alice Friedman, Wellesley College, USA

Paul Groth, University of California at Berkeley, USA

Craig Gurney, Cardiff University, UK

Ian Hodder, Stanford University, USA

Home Cultures is indexed by ARTbibliographies Modern (http://www.csa.com) and MLA International Bibliography.

Printed in the UK by Henry Ling Ltd, Dorchester

HOME CULTURES
VOLUME 1
ISSUE 2
JULY 2004

CONTENTS

HOME CULTURES   VOLUME 1, ISSUE 2. PP 89–126

MÉLANIE VAN DER HOORN

CONSUMING THE "PLATTE" IN EAST BERLIN: THE NEW POPULARITY OF FORMER GDR ARCHITECTURE

MÉLANIE VAN DER HOORN STUDIED CULTURAL ANTHROPOLOGY AT THE UNIVERSITY OF AMSTERDAM. SHE IS CURRENTLY FINISHING HER PHD "INDISPENSABLE EYESORES. AN ANTHROPOLOGY OF UNDESIRED ARCHITECTURE," AT UTRECHT UNIVERSITY, WITH CASE STUDIES IN GERMANY, AUSTRIA, HUNGARY, AND BOSNIA-HERZEGOVINA.

This article is an analysis of the social and cultural relevance of alternative attitudes towards contested architecture. A concrete example is given by the so-called "Plattenbauten" in East Berlin, prefabricated apartment blocks erected during GDR times, many of which are currently reported to be unoccupied. In the media, they are often extremely negatively portrayed and associated with anonymity, criminality, and right-wing radicalism. Despite this, in the late 1990s, living in the "Platte" gained a new kind of popularity when many young designers, architects, and artists decided to live and/ or work there.

These newcomers have no formal responsibility or influence in city planning matters: they are not policy makers, city planners, or investors. Nevertheless, by consuming the Plattenbauten and stimulating others to do the same, they are able to shed new light on these buildings and to create new images. Their attitude towards the Plattenbauten is analyzed from various perspectives: the appreciation and presentation of architecture from within as an efficient strategy to counter negative images; detachment as a necessary condition for the commodification of generally undesired architecture; differences between images "at a distance," "at eye level" and "from within" as different attitudes towards the history from which specific buildings emerged; and cultural gentrification as a means of appropriating (images of) other people's architecture. The analysis is clearly focused on the attitude of the newcomers but other viewpoints, such as those of the original tenants, are also described, as far as they contrast or cause friction with the newcomers' approaches.

In East Berlin and, more generally, in East Germany, hundreds of thousands of former German Democratic Republic (GDR) high-rise buildings—so-called "Plattenbauten," prefabricated apartment blocks—are reported to be unoccupied. Erected within a few decades to make, literally and figuratively, socialist dreams and ideals concrete, these apartments embodied comfort, high standards and modernity during GDR times—people were on a waiting list for several years to get one. After German reunification, their reputation changed drastically, as reported, notably, in the media. People with enough income preferred to move to a single-family dwelling in the countryside, and smaller towns lost their *raison d'être* when the industrial complexes with which they were connected were closed. Simone Hain, an architectural historian specializing in East German socialist architecture, summarizes the situation as follows:

> The great utopia which [. . .] inspired the architects of the GDR [. . .] was the collective search for a perfect system of prefabrication as an efficient means of managing resources and making work easier for all trades involved in construction: intelligent complex planning, easy assembly to save time and energy and "more than comfortable" spatial organization of family and community life. However, this fully industrialized means of ecological production in the GDR, which is generally classed as "Plattenbau," is now often regarded as an expression of a spiteful left-wing Fordist instrumentalism. As a spatial system determined by shortage and deficit management (Hain 2003: 80).

In Berlin, vacancy rates in non-renovated GDR apartments vary between one-seventh and one-third (Geisel 2002: 30). In total, in East

Germany, about one million apartments are empty. In several towns, vacancy rates have become so problematic that certain buildings have had to be torn down. In the media, these areas are extremely negatively portrayed and currently associated with anonymity, criminality, and right-wing radicalism.[1] In a sociological study for Humboldt University about the revaluation of Plattenbauten, Awuku *et al.* (2001) describe their reputation with the following words:

> Plattenbauten: grey, ugly concrete monstrosities, the cold and silent witnesses of another age. Monotone stone deserts, into which even the extensive renovations of the past few years could not breathe new life. The flight away from the Platte cannot be stopped. "Only dynamite could help that now", tearing down and "renaturation" are all that's left (Awuku *et al.* 2001: 3) (Figure 1).[2]

Nicknames such as "rabbit hutch," "shoebox" or "locker for workers" are very common (Rietdorf 1997: 7). While it is not often necessary (yet) in Berlin for buildings to be eliminated, nevertheless the existence of Plattenbauten is severely questioned and, as Geisel (2002) puts it

Figure 1
Cartoon by Gerd Wessel:
"Platte away—problems away!?"

in a recent article about Hellersdorf, a peripheral district of East Berlin: "No other building type is so defamed in public as the so-called Plattenbau" (Geisel 2002: 29).

Despite all this, a series of articles appeared at the end of the 1990s, first in design and architecture magazines, and later in the regular press, with titles such as: "Honi's Platte is Hip Again" (Honi is short for Erich Honecker), "Living in the Platte is Absolutely Trendy" or "New Life in the (C)old Platte."[3] Indeed, in the late 1990s many young designers, architects, and artists decided to live and/or work in Plattenbauten or other former GDR architecture. Some of them also furnished their apartments with designs from the 1960s and 1970s. These were portrayed in glossy magazines. A famous German pop group, *Echt*, used one of these apartments as a location for a music video. Perhaps the most ironic thing is that capitalist firms like Coca-Cola, Mövenpick, Vodafone, and Volkswagen filmed commercials in these backdrops of socialist realism (Figure 2).

What does the new popularity of former GDR architecture—Plattenbauten in particular—tell us about the social and cultural relevance of alternative attitudes towards contested architecture? This article is part of a larger investigation into the significance of undesired architecture,

Figure 2
An empty Plattenbau in Halle-Neustadt transformed into a hip hotel for several weeks.

i.e. buildings (or projects) whose existence is publicly questioned and sometimes physically altered by people who have, or took, the power to do so. In my research, entitled "Indispensable Eyesores," I draw upon various case studies in Germany, Austria, Hungary, and Bosnia-Herzegovina to examine how, and why, various groups of people alter what they consider to be undesired architecture. To paraphrase Daniel Miller in his "Introduction" to *Material Cultures. Why Some Things Matter* (1998), I address the question of why undesired architecture "matters." This term "puts the burden of mattering clearly on evidence of concern to those being discussed" (Miller 1998: 11).

In the "Introduction" to his *An Archaeology of Socialism* (2000), Victor Buchli writes that: "Of all the material cultures produced by societies, architecture is probably the most durable, long-lasting and easily retrievable. Architecture is also the material cultural matrix which most other artefacts of material culture are associated with or related to" (Buchli 2000: 1). This partly explains why questioning a building's existence—unexpectedly emphasizing the ephemerality of something supposedly durable—has such relevance and contributes to what David Crowley calls "peaks of dramatic transformation or troughs of controversy," as opposed to "level history" (Crowley 2002: 202). Architecture, understood as material culture, can undergo various destinies: a building, or group of buildings, can be eliminated, transformed or only challenged. Depending on the question of whether the other individuals involved approve the rejection of a so-called "eyesore" or not, the situation gains various meanings. When people agree with each other that a building has to be eliminated, for example, demolition can be given the character of a collective, secular sacrifice.[4] When various groups of people disagree about the building's fate, and all have power and influence in such debates—because of their profession or political position, or simply because of their number—then this can give rise to long-lasting discussions in which they confront their images together. Finally, it may be that some individuals who feel concerned about the fate of the building do not have enough official power to be able to influence such matters. In this situation, the only possible means to counteract the dominant perception and decision-making is by arguing on another level. The revival of GDR architecture in Berlin is an example of the latter situation.

Newcomers, who perceive the Plattenbauten from a different viewpoint than the predominantly negative public image, have no formal responsibility or influence in city planning matters: they are not policy makers, city planners, or investors. They can only witness urban developments and decision-making processes without being able to influence them directly. Nevertheless, by consuming the Plattenbauten and stimulating others to do the same, they are able to shed new light on these buildings and to create new images. The relation between consumption and cultural identification—self-construction and self-presentation, in particular—has been discussed by various authors.[5] More specifically with regard to architecture, Caroline Humphrey has insisted that: "Consumption is central to the creation of culture, since it involves a process of objectification which enables material things and their discourses to become forms through which people have consciousness of themselves" (Humphrey 2002: 176). We will see that these remarks apply particularly well to the newcomers in the Plattenbauten. Humphrey's chapter "The Villas of the 'New Russians': A Sketch of Consumption and Cultural Identity in Post-Soviet Landscapes" presents other interesting parallels with observations that can be made in East Berlin. In her conclusion, she agrees with Daniel Miller that "the authentic culture of modern urban people may be created out of faked or recycled images," but she adds that there must be certain conditions for this to happen. On the one hand: "There must be a resilience and energy given to image making itself." And on the other hand: "there must be the possibility of rather direct appropriation of material objects to the process of identification" (Humphrey 2002: 200). In East Berlin, with regard to the Plattenbauten, both of these conditions were met. Generally, buildings are among the most difficult pieces of material culture to appropriate, but when they tend to be rejected as undesirable elements, it makes them at the same time much more accessible.

The newcomers' attitude towards the Plattenbauten as well as their tendency for image making, form the central focus in this article, as an example of an alternative point of view on rejected architecture. Their innovative and detached approach is influenced by a complex intermingling of historic backgrounds, personal identifications, and cultural affinities: most newcomers are West Berliners, West Germans, or Western Europeans in their twenties or thirties, working in the arts, architecture or design. In order to uncover how they alter the (image of the) Plattenbauten as well as why these buildings matter, several questions were posed: Are the newcomers' images related to the inside, the outside, and/or the surroundings of the buildings? In what way do they consume the Plattenbauten? Are they totally indifferent to the history from which this architecture emerged? Is the appreciation of former GDR architecture just a (temporary) trend, or is it indicative of a changed perception of this architecture? Did the newcomers really appropriate the (images of the) "Platte?"

Newcomers are not the only ones with a positive perception of the Plattenbauten: some of the original tenants are still very attached to their domestic environment, which they would not like to be demolished. In the last few years, their individual experiences have tended to be described more often in daily newspapers.[6] Nevertheless, they have not formed an organized group, actively fighting to "restore the good name of the Plattenbauten," nor do the media present their perception as something new, that would contribute to a changed attitude towards these buildings. Rather, they embody some kind of continuity in a context of unprecedented social and political change. They are sociologically, politically, and economically relevant by their number, but they do not explicitly partake in the forum about the future of the Plattenbauten. Their attitude will mainly be described as far as it contrasts or causes friction with the newcomers' approaches.

In her chapter about the villas of the New Russians, Caroline Humphrey has emphasized the "difficulty and contingency of identification as a process," especially when it occurs "through the medium of large material objects like houses, which are subject to economic, political, and other constraints and always sit in a landscape created by other interests and histories" (Humphrey 2002: 182). When buildings are demolished or transformed, this ambiguity of identification through architecture is sometimes obscured by the univocality of the act. But when a building remains untouched despite its negative reputation, this ambiguity—which makes it all the more interesting—becomes much more apparent.

EYESORES FROM WITHIN

In *Thought Styles: Critical Essays on Good Taste* (1996), Mary Douglas writes: "The discourse about dislike and ugliness is more revealing than the discourse about aesthetic beauty" (Douglas 1996: 50). Our first focus will be on the descriptions made by the voluntary new users of GDR architecture: What do they tell us about these buildings, which are considered repulsive by the majority of people? Do they have a different taste, or do they, perhaps, consider aesthetic aspects unimportant or secondary? Douglas further writes: "To know why people do consume, we need to understand why they sometimes do not" (Douglas 1996: 107). Here we need to analyze a double refusal: the apparently dominant rejection of GDR architecture (at least in the media) on the one hand, and the positive valuation of these buildings by a minority of people on the other—implying a refusal of the architecture appreciated by the majority.

For most newcomers in the Plattenbauten (and in GDR architecture, in general), it was a coincidence that they moved into these buildings to live or work—they heard about the accommodation from friends or read an advertisement in the newspaper. There were, probably, a few criteria that their new home had to meet in any case, but they had no previous knowledge, no clear expectations nor prejudices concerning the specific buildings into which they would soon move. For example, Erik Schmidt, an artist who lives on the eleventh floor of a Plattenbau on the Platz der Vereinten Nationen, recalls that he had never heard of that address before:[7] "It just gave 'United Nations Square' as the address, and I didn't know that location, what it was or what the neighbourhood was like. But the address and the description appealed to me. It stated 'maisonette' or 'five rooms' and it was cheap, I found it all fascinating" (Figure 3).

Most people explained their decision to move in as an unbiased, positive valuation of the architectural object itself, without really considering the direct environment, the historic or symbolic meaning

Figure 3
Erik Schmidt's apartment: bare walls, minimalist furniture, neutral colors, with a few colored accents.

of the place or the potential neighbors. For these young people—many of them from West Berlin or West Germany—the rent seemed afford-able, and the place was a very welcome alternative to the non-renovated Altbau: apartments from the first half of the twentieth century, dark, with a shared toilet in the corridor and a coal stove instead of central heat-ing. The contrast between these two types of accommodation, which already existed during GDR times, was emphasized by almost all the people I spoke with.

If Plattenbauten are as luxurious as these people assert, then why do they have such a negative reputation? Firstly, their aesthetic aspects certainly do not work in their favor. Even in the book *Peripherie als Ort. Das Hellersdorfer Projekt* (1999), which was meant to shed a more sensitive light on Hellersdorf, a residential district built in the periphery of East Berlin in the 1980s, Rolf Schneider starts his article with the following description:

> It starts with a glacis of empty space, unkempt plains with few trees, just behind this the new buildings come into view. They appear cold, massive, rejecting witnesses of an entirely different world, trumpeting their presence and stifling all memories of the sub-divisions of an old Berlin suburb (Schneider 1999: 93).

In the first chapter of a book entitled *Weiter wohnen in der Platte. Probleme der Weiterentwicklung großer Neubauwohngebiete in den neuen Bundesländern* (1997), the editor Werner Rietdorf gives a clear and structured overview of the problems and potentials of various Plattenbauten districts in East Germany. He admits that many of them are relatively small and standardized in comparison with their Western counterparts, that many of them have construction faults such as leaking roofs or dysfunctioning sanitary installations, and that there is a general lack of commercial and service infrastructure in these districts (Rietdorf 1997: 31). He also warns, however, against generalization and pleads for a differentiated approach to various types of buildings, erected in different places and different periods. Finally, it must be added that the situation with prefabricated apartment blocks changed radically in certain areas in the 1990s. More specifically, some of these areas lost their purpose when industrial complexes were closed. In addition, some people preferred to move to the countryside. With the disappearance of the strong social structures that existed before German reunification, many of these areas have become so-called dormitory suburbs: people go to town to work, shop, and enjoy culture, and they go to the countryside for recreation.

Nevertheless, the negative reputation of these areas is also largely influenced by Western perception and reporting. In Western Europe, prefabricated apartment blocks are constructed for people with a relatively low socioeconomic status. These areas are often characterized by high unemployment rates, social problems, and criminality. Several respondents emphasized that prefabricated apartment blocks in the GDR were constructed with a totally different intention, to solve the housing shortage after the Second World War as quickly as possible, in an egalitarian way. The population in these flats was relatively mixed— certain blocks even represented an elite, because loyal citizens (productive workers, zealous civil servants, professors) had better chances of obtaining an apartment from the State. According to Werner Rietdorf, this "healthy social mix" (Rietdorf 1997: 33) still persists nowadays and is complemented by an increasing variation in terms of age structure. Sieglinde Geisel mentions in her article about Hellersdorf that the term "Plattenbau" is a Western invention that obscures the positive reputation of these buildings in former East Berlin:[8] "No-one living there called it Platte" (Geisel 2002: 30). And she quotes the mayor of Hellersdorf: "We called them total-comfort accommodation, because we were fascinated that warm water came out of the tap." Even nowadays, more than 50% of the inhabitants in East Berlin are living in prefabricated apartment blocks, and more than 80% of them are reported to be satisfied.[9] Many blocks still need to be renovated, but Werner Rietdorf writes that in-depth analyses of the state of these buildings has proved their durability, as well as the technical and financial feasibility to renovate them, or even structurally modernize them (Rietdorf 1997: 38). Peripheral districts such as Hellersdorf or Marzahn, with many prefabricated apartment blocks, are already mainly characterized by order and tidiness, as noted by Axel Watzke, a student in design communication who organized a large-scale artistic project in a Plattenbau in the Summer of 2002: "Hellersdorf is a very middle-class area, extremely well looked after, with front gardens like allotments. The cliché of ghetto really doesn't apply there." Sieglinde Geisel emphasizes the *petit-bourgeois* character of Hellersdorf: "The 'Club of Garden Inspectors' are honorary caretakers of tidy courtyards; graffiti is removed by the caretaker every two weeks. Curtains hang in the windows, artfully gathered, lace trimming and decoratively divided" (Geisel 2002: 30).

Most importantly, prefabricated apartment blocks should not all be put in the same category. First of all, in Berlin, a significant number of them were built in or near the city center. Naturally, these apartments allow easy access to the rich and complex infrastructure of the inner districts and a different lifestyle from that in the dormitory suburbs. In addition, although all Plattenbauten look very similar at first sight and were supposed to embody egalitarian housing, there are nevertheless some significant differences in standard: if most centrally located blocks are well equipped, and some of them have even been renovated, certain eighteen-story buildings in Marzahn do not even have an elevator. It must be added that newcomers in the Plattenbauten have all chosen centrally located buildings; they would probably not make the move to a peripheral district.

People who recently moved into GDR architecture to live or work were not influenced by the negative reputation of these buildings. Dominant negative images of architecture are often based on its outside appearance or its symbolic meaning—seldom on an appreciation of its inner space. Zohlen (1999: 138) writes that stereotypical portrayals of the Plattenbauten often result from an abstract and distant viewpoint, as from a helicopter or on a drawing table.[10] An evaluation of the inside of a building requires a more thorough investigation, and it cannot be so easily subjugated to generalizing statements or prejudices. In a chapter entitled "Existence, location and function: The appreciation of architecture" (1994), Allen Carlson describes a so-called "path of appreciation:" "In approaching, we experience a work's existence, in closing and circling, we experience its outer form and its fit with its site, and, lastly, upon entering, we experience the fit between its outer and inner space and experientially realize its function" (Carlson 1994: 160). For an in-depth judgment of architecture, it is thus necessary to enter the building and to get a feeling for how it functions. Newcomers in the Plattenbauten looked beyond stereotypes and ready-made perceptions to judge the architecture on its own merit. If they had responded to the dominant reputation of this architecture on a similar level of superficiality—by setting another distant and superficial image against it—their approach would not have received as much attention. Indeed, Sharon Zukin has elucidated in a chapter about "Space and Symbols in an Age of Decline" (1996) that the rights of disposal over a certain place include the rights of disposal over its image, its symbolic dimension: "To ask 'Whose city?' suggests more than a politics of occupation; it also asks who has a right to inhabit the dominant image of the city" (Zukin 1996: 43). Clearly, the newcomers in the Plattenbauten have no official influence on city planning matters and no "right to inhabit the dominant image of the city." The only means for them to eventually contribute to a changed perception of the Plattenbauten is by entering them and letting other people enter them as well: opening up these buildings, i.e. the objects themselves, leaving their outside appearance and symbolic connotations aside, and showing their potential. If this was not initially the intention of the new Plattenbau users—they moved in for purely pragmatic and personal reasons—it was, however, the result of their actions.

This is not to say that newcomers are the first ones to appreciate the inner space of the Plattenbauten, but their approach is innovative in that they also consciously open them up and purposely make the private realm public. Traditionally, despite—or perhaps precisely because of—the efforts of socialist states to penetrate and publicize the private sphere, inhabitants were experiencing and dealing with public and private spaces in remarkably different ways. In a book entitled *Wohnkultur und Plattenbau. Beispiele aus Berlin und Budapest* (1994), Kerstin Dörhöfer writes that what inhabitants dislike the most about their domestic environment is the lack of flexibility and the exterior design. Displaying personal creativity, they try to counterbalance the excessive standardization and create a warm and cosy interior by means of a distinctive arrangement of furniture and personal belongings (Dörhöfer 1994: 201). Other authors confirm that the antithesis between private and public space characterized Eastern-bloc countries for many years. The effort that people put into the conception of their homes was much more than purely a question of taste; it was a means of identification through the appropriation of material culture and space.[11] The most concrete description of people's attachment to their domestic space in this context is provided by Adam Drazin with regard to Romanian interiors. In the "Introduction" to *Home Possessions: Material Culture behind Closed Doors* (2001) Miller announces Drazin's analysis as follows:

> The startling aesthetic contrast between the grey and crumbling concrete of Soviet-system blocks of flats with the emphasis on wooden furniture and infrastructure within their warm interiors, objectifies two histories: that of the public and the state on the one hand and a domestic situation that has tried to reconstitute itself in defiance of the constraints that were imposed (Miller 2001: 13).

Certain newcomers were soon confronted with the special meaning that private space had acquired during several decades of GDR. When Ulli Uphaus, a young landscape architect, moved into his apartment on the fifteenth floor of a Plattenbau in the Leipzigerstraße, he intended to organize an art exhibition on all floors of the twenty-five-story building. A renowned local artist was willing to produce new paintings for this occasion, which would be exhibited in each of the apartments at places chosen by the occupants themselves. Uphaus contacted all of his neighbors, presented them with a detailed concept for the project . . . and received no more than two responses (both negative).

For the original tenants, their apartments constitute a place of escape from or protest against the public realm. For the newcomers, on the contrary, they form a means to be immersed in the latter. They appreciate the interiors of the Plattenbauten for different reasons: they not only consider the infrastructure largely superior to that of the Altbauten, but also praise the quality of the rooms in terms of light and space. (We should be aware, however, that apartments in which entire families were living are now occupied by two new inhabitants at the most.) Erik Schmidt explained to me that he had completely different expectations when he moved to Berlin and that the Plattenbauten turned out to be a surprisingly pleasant discovery:

> I didn't like old Berlin, the city was closed off and nothing ever happened and the people were slow. When you visited friends there, you always sat in a dark basement or ground floor flat, and it was cold. We didn't know the architecture of the Plattenbauten, they were locked up, so after the Wall fell they were the only new bit left to explore, so to speak. [. . .] And now you are high up, the sun shines, there is light there.

One of the main differences in perception between the inside and outside of these apartments is that what makes them unattractive at first sight—their large size and uniformity—enhances the quality of their inner space in terms of light and a spectacular view of the city. For Ulli Uphaus, the main motivation for moving into his apartment was the height. He definitely wanted to live in a high-rise building—"the higher, the better"—and this one turned up by coincidence. Another landscape architect, Frank Peter Thomas, who lives on the twentieth floor of another tower in the same street, explained to me that the proportions of the apartment—relatively long drawn-out rooms with low ceilings—give him the impression of being in a bungalow, floating over the city somewhere around the twentieth floor. If Plattenbauten are perhaps not particularly attractive from the outside, their inhabitants have found the best strategy to avoid this view: by experiencing them from the inside and enjoying what they can offer. In his essay on "The Eiffel Tower" (1997 [1964]), Roland Barthes remarked:

> In order to negate the Eiffel Tower [. . .] you must [. . .] get up on it and, so to speak, identify yourself with it. Like man himself, who is the only one not to know his own glance, the Tower

is the only blind point of the total optical system of which it is the centre and Paris the circumference. But in this movement which seems to limit it, the Tower acquires a new power: an object when we look at it, it becomes a lookout in its turn when we visit it, and now constitutes as an object, simultaneously extended and collected beneath it, that Paris which just now was looking at it (Barthes 1997 [1964]: 173).

In other words, from inside the towers, people gain access or another relationship to the city. An Altbau apartment may be attractive to some people for its high ceilings and wooden floors, but it is generally a relatively closed space. High-rise buildings, on the other hand, allow a much more "urban" experience, as several respondents described to me; inhabitants have the feeling of being in the midst of town (Figure 4). Frank Peter Thomas described this feeling in a comparison between two of his working places, the former in an Altbau, the latter in the so-called Haus des Lehrers on the Alexanderplatz. This very prominent building was designed by GDR architect Hermann Henselmann and used for teacher training. It remained empty for many years after German reunification, until it was put into use again by a number of artists, architects, and designers in the late 1990s. Frank Peter Thomas recalls the contrast with his previous working place:

> Before when we were in that flat, with coal heating, somewhere in a courtyard, you couldn't see anything, it was simply a room in which you worked. But then at the Alexanderplatz, it was completely different, very urban. We had large windows, we were located far down, on the first floor, we were involved in the traffic. Nevertheless, we had a great view, because the house is on the corner and you can look down on the railway, and watch the high-speed trains come and go from the station. This is really big city life, tons of traffic on the street, accidents always happening, there was always something to see on the street. Next door was the Congress Hall. Once a month they held an erotic fair, we could see the posters, it was a colourful scene, very interesting. [. . .] We let ourselves be inspired by the atmosphere there, the prospect and the view of the street in the middle of the city, the urbanity of Berlin.

The direct experience of the urban environment—feeling part of the city—constitutes a discovery for the new users of this architecture; some of them even refer to it as a real "liberation."[12] All this also illustrates how much the dominant—here, negative—reputation of a building or type of building can be disconnected from a close and real appreciation of its inner space. When people are not influenced by the dominant attitudes, they can approach a building without prejudice and experience the architecture for itself. This is perhaps the most effective way to counter negative images.

Figure 4
The view from Ulli Uphaus's apartment: being in the midst of town.

The newcomers' attitude towards their homes does more than diverge from that of the original tenants in that the former have blurred the fundamental border between public and private, whereas the latter would tend to emphasize it. They also clearly have different conceptions and expectations of domestic environments. In her analysis of Plattenbauten interiors in Berlin and Budapest, Kerstin Dörhöfer has systematically inventoried aspects of middle-class, modern, and postmodern home cultures. She writes that a large majority of tenants displays a predominantly middle-class home culture, in which home, understood as a place for relaxation and as a status symbol, is unmistakably associated with the family, as opposed to the larger community. Aspects of modern and postmodern home cultures are also present, but they are certainly not predominant. In the former, home is conceived as an extension of the larger, increasingly industrialized community and characterized by functionalism and rationality. In the latter, home embodies individuality and a personal interpretation of the larger community; objects are no longer granted a meaning by their function, but by what people symbolically associate with them. This description applies to the new inhabitants' conceptions of home: they do appreciate their apartments, and they would not like to move out (at least, not for the moment), but, in general, they present their apartments as temporary, utilitarian objects that can be exchanged for more suitable ones if needed or wanted. In magazines, the images of their apartments are not those of intimacy and individual biographies, i.e. their homes are not primarily presented as places for privacy, refuge, security or self-identity, but mainly as cult objects, as models or stages. "These homes are cool," seems to be the message; "and so are the people living there." This can be illustrated by a photo series in *Esquire*,[13] an architecture and design magazine, in which Erik Schmidt's apartment has been compared to that of his neighbors, who came to live there in GDR times. Bare walls, minimalist furniture, and neutral colors—except for a few colored accents—characterize Schmidt's apartment. Schmidt knew from the very beginning what the place should look like (Figure 5). At the end of the 1990s, design and fashion from the 1960s and 1970s had already become trendy, but not the corresponding architecture. When he visited the apartment for the first time, he knew at first sight that it could become like a place in the architecture and design magazine *Wallpaper*. In his *Homestory: A Glimpse of a Modern Artist's Living* (2002)[14] he presented a series of consciously styled photos with comments on the character of the place. He described the transformation as follows:

> The space in the protected historical monument Plattenbau group presented the ideal possibility for contemporary living. In furniture the artist chooses modern design, which incorporates the accent of the Sixties and corresponds to the character of the building. Minimal investment would emphasise the object-like quality of the interior. At relevant positions the original

Figure 5
"A glimpse of a modern artist's living:" Erik Schmidt's apartment.

condition would be restored: while in the entrance way the original wallpaper would be exposed, in other rooms the concrete walls would be visible. Their materiality and colour are highly stimulating (Schmidt and Weidner 2002).

The neighbors' apartment is not only totally different in style, but also much more loaded with personal objects and meanings. It contains much more furniture—including some heavy, dark wooden cupboards—and is largely decorated with paintings, plants, figurines, carpets, and paraphernalia: all kinds of objects that embody people's occupation of, and relation to, the place. Pictures of the neighbor's home clearly show personal attachment.

CONSUMING THE EYESORES

After their first contact with the Plattenbauten or other GDR architecture, new users realized that these buildings were not only suitable for personal use but could be further consumed if they were transformed into something new, mediatized and merchandized. As soon as Schmidt's apartment was ready, he produced a video film and a series of postcards and offered it as a location for rent to an advertising agency. The main motivation for doing this is the awareness that images of the apartment could attract a good price: "Naturally, that had a lot to do with capitalism, to say: I have something here, that is my potential, how can I market it." The ice-cream brand Mövenpick was the first to rent Schmidt's apartment as a location for a commercial; the income was enough for Schmidt to pay a few months' rent (Lüdtke 2002: 62). Other commercials and publications soon followed. With the title "Platte putzen" ("Cleaning Platte"), *Max* presented four newcomers in the Plattenbauten along with images of their interiors. *Home* followed with "Neues Leben in der (k)alten Platte" ("New Life in the (C)old Platte"): interviews with four inhabitants, illustrated by glossy pictures of their trendy homes. Many other magazines and newspapers reported on the same theme in the following months. *Der Spiegel* published an in-depth report entitled "Dufte urban" ("Great Urban"), and the new trend even reached the other side of the Atlantic with one-page coverage in *The New York Times*, stating that: "In chic new Berlin, ugly is way cool."[15] In the following period, Coca-Cola, Volkswagen, and Vodafone used Schmidt's apartment or other Plattenbauten as locations for commercials. *Echt*, a German pop group for teenagers, made a music video in which Schmidt's apartment appears in its true state, very recognizable, with several views of the surroundings. Schmidt recalls that it was very special to see groups of teenagers in front of the door, waiting for an autograph from their idols. Indeed, the target group of this German-speaking band lives in the Plattenbauten; to them this architecture is not strange, but familiar: "It is of course very special that their favourite group suddenly has come to live, so to speak, in the same architecture that they live in, which can have a negative reputation."

The newcomers' apparent detachment from the more intimate and personal aspects of home was a necessary condition to make images of the Plattenbauten suitable for the media. Commercials, video clips, and magazines do not primarily aim at rewriting the history or ideological background of the Plattenbauten, nor do they subtly affect collective stereotypes by means of the personal experiences of old and new inhabitants. Rather, they present images of the architectural objects in themselves, their qualities and potentialities. Representations of people's attachment to their homes as private, intimate spaces would just not sell. In Marzahn and Hellersdorf, great effort was made—supported by big investments—to renovate Plattenbauten and differentiate them from each other by means of individual balconies, artworks on the roof, plants, and colored or decorated facades. Although this corresponds, for many people, to a positive image of the Plattenbauten, it has never received—and will never receive—the same attention as the apartments mentioned before. Gerd Wessel, architect, artist and cartoonist, ironically focuses on these spruced-up buildings in his cartoons. He questions the superficiality of these initiatives, which fail to deal with the architectural objects themselves, and ridicules their *petit-bourgeois* character. In order to open up the Plattenbauten and make people aware of their potential, they need to be freed of connotations to intimacy and individual experiences of home—people must be able to project their own ideals and wishes on them.

Detachment is not only necessary to the mediatizing, but also to the merchandizing of Plattenbauten and other GDR architecture. Indeed, one could say that these buildings went through a process of commoditization. Before German reunification, commoditization was restricted, meaning that many things were "not exchangeable and not for sale," to paraphrase Igor Kopytoff in his chapter "The Cultural Biography of Things: Commoditization as Process" (1986). More specifically, most people had to be on a waiting list for years to obtain an apartment. Things changed drastically in the 1990s as newcomers could easily move into the Plattenbauten. Nevertheless, history can explain why the people who already lived there did not necessarily appreciate their arrival. Ulli Uphaus, for example, had the following impression:

> Several people on this floor are a little eccentric, they've been living here for 30 years, forever. You notice sometimes that they feel: people come here from the west or young people, turn the music up loud and perhaps ignore the neighbours a bit. They feel rather like they have priority here because they've lived here so long and they had to apply to get a flat here. While for us it was so easy to find a place here.

The situation was even more striking in the apartment block were Erik Schmidt lives: some of his neighbors were opposed to his initiative to rent his apartment as a location. They went to the rent tribunal and obtained a ban on further filming. Schmidt explained their resistance to me as a lack of economic awareness due to several decades under a communist regime, where profit seeking was negatively valued. I would rather say, along the line of Zukin's remarks about "who has a right to inhabit the dominant image of the city," that the original inhabitants had the feeling that (the image of) their home was appropriated by people who did not have that right. Indeed, Werner Rietdorf has emphasized that in GDR times, the State granted people a guarantee on their apartment, which was thus like a social good, completely independent of their financial situation. Therefore, people's attachment to rented apartments was remarkably strong and durable—people identified with them as if they owned them. Inhabitants were even willing to renovate both private and communal spaces at their own expense (Rietdorf 1997: 35–6).[16] This explains why the world of these residents simply clashed with that of the advertising managers from Hamburg, who occupied all the parking places with their Jaguars and thought that money gave them the right to rule the place for the day. Caroline Humphrey describes a similar situation in her analysis of the villas of the New Russians. Focusing on the contradictory and contested character of identifications through the means of architectural objects, she insists that groups of people who are excluded from but nevertheless feel concerned by, these processes can contribute to undermining the meanings and images embodied by these buildings: "The construction of a public exterior [. . .] that excludes others is also the shining face on which the excluded inscribe their envy, jealousy, admiration, and so forth" (Humphrey 2002: 182).

The conflict between the pragmatic, sometimes profit-seeking attitude of the newcomers on the one hand, and the resistance of former GDR citizens against these developments on the other, can be interpreted as an opposition between commoditization and singularization, as defined by Kopytoff. Indeed, mediatizing and merchandizing make GDR architecture "exchangeable or for sale" (Kopytoff 1986: 69); this is a process of commoditization. Newcomers have a detached attitude to GDR architecture: they approach these buildings as objects in themselves, because of their functional qualities and their relatively cheap price. When benefits can be made, they do not hesitate to merchandise this architecture, which then becomes a product among others on the worldwide market. Erik Schmidt was not the only one who realized that his apartment could become a source of income if rented to advertising agencies. Similarly, the great interest displayed by the print media was also involved with an economic awareness: residents charged magazines for taking photos, and apartments were presented among other architecture or design pieces, not primarily for contemplative or reflexive purposes, but as something that other consumers could potentially acquire as well. In the same period, GDR architecture was introduced into the club scene, as Gerriet Schulz, creative director of the WMF-Club[17] explained to me. There was a sudden revival of the aesthetics of Plattenbau facades: a Plattenbau happy families game was created, and facade elements were used for the design of flyers and in the form of video projections (Figure 6). The WMF Club got hold of the entire interior of the Palast der Republik and other buildings as well, including some high-quality technical equipment which they could otherwise never have afforded.

Through all these developments, GDR architecture has been commercialized and has gained an economic value. Nevertheless, Gerriet Schulz also explained to me that especially elderly people from the former GDR were not necessarily happy with these developments. He recalled the comments of the caretaker in the building of the Council of State, where Schulz and others presented projects for the Palast der Republik:

> He said to me: he would prefer to tear the thing down before some obscure artist got up to pranks with the GDR architecture. Better to go down with honour than end up a ruin of GDR architecture that someone plays with. There are many former GDR inhabitants who mourn the passing of the old state, who fulfilled positions of importance, they don't like what we are doing. They would prefer it to be torn down, over and done with, than have drugs consumed here, young people, etc.

Figure 6
The WMF-Club in Café Moskau: one of the trendiest clubs in town.

Kopytoff has written that: "The counterdrive to [the] potential onrush of commoditization is culture" (Kopytoff 1986: 73). Indeed, for those who resist commoditization, GDR architecture has not only functional characteristics, but also—mainly—an important historic and symbolic value; it reminds them of a historical period in which their cultural identity is rooted. They have lived for several decades in a state where apartments were "publicly precluded from being commoditized" (p. 73). Not only do people need some time to get used to, and eventually accept, the changed perception of buildings as commodities, even when they recognize the commodity status of architecture, this does not stop the simultaneous processes of singularization: "[. . .] even things that unambiguously carry an exchange value—formally speaking, therefore, commodities—do absorb the other kind of worth, one that is nonmonetary and goes beyond exchange worth" (p. 83).

These remarks apply not only to the so-called DDR-Sonderbauten (special buildings), but to residential districts as well: as the Plattenbauten are very recent in terms of architectural history, many current residents were the very first ones to move into their apartments—they were, so to say, "pioneers," and this creates a special kind of attachment between fellow inhabitants, and to the place. Wolfgang Kil has emphasized this in his article "Eine Stadt wie jede andere" (1999), where he writes that this is almost incomprehensible for people who have always lived in historic architecture:

> As the difficult beginning in construction rubble and the lack of incomplete infrastructure, thus the local timeless "zero hour," acted to a great extent especially forming identity and thus individual history, the inhabitants of old cities are seldom aware and thus cannot understand what sort of motivation stimulates those people "out there." As the positive creation myths of the inhabitants of the new cities were denigrated and turned around as part of the system change, the crisis of identity in these regions increased massively (Kil 1999).

The attachment to GDR architecture makes it very difficult to look at the buildings as objects in themselves—disconnected from personal or historic meanings—and thus to present them and/or sell them as such. Thus, we could say that in order to create positive images of the Plattenbauten that are not on the same level of superficiality as their negative counterparts and also have the potential to become meaningful to an increasing number of people, it is necessary to approach them from within and to share these images with others without imprinting personal values on them.

EYESORES AND HISTORY

The different relationship of newcomers and former GDR citizens to GDR architecture can also be illustrated by the situation in the Haus des Lehrers. Upon their arrival in the building, one of the first discoveries the incoming tenants made was the porter. Twenty-four hours a day, someone was sitting at the entrance to guard the place and manage the keys. When tenants wanted to go into their office, they had to sign in to get their key; when leaving the building, they had to check out. Most of them liked this system; they saw it as part of the highly functional and convenient infrastructure of this freshly discovered architecture. There was no risk of losing or forgetting one's key, and it gave them a feeling of security. Frank Peter Thomas told me, however, that there were also a few tenants who had grown up in the GDR, who did not appreciate this system at all. It reminded them of the extreme and regular controls in GDR times, which imposed severe restrictions on individual freedom.[18] Similarly, Gerriet Schulz told me that although the regular customers of the WMF-Club were, from the beginning, from both East and West Germany, not all of them appreciated the introduction of GDR aesthetics in the interior design. Some East Germans complained: "I don't want to go to a club and be surrounded by the shit I grew up with." These differences in perception raise the question of whether the attitude of newcomers towards GDR architecture is really entirely disconnected from its history. Furthermore, we may ask to what extent a positive valuation of generally undesired architecture such as the Plattenbauten can remain completely ahistoric.

Most new users of GDR architecture told me that they were not really aware of the history from which it had emerged when they moved in, but they soon developed a consciousness for the place in which they were living or working. Ulli Uphaus said that he soon got the feeling that the Haus des Lehrers was extremely "pregnant with history." It was mainly the discovery of the architectural object from within which aroused the newcomers' curiosity for the corresponding history. Rob Savelberg, a young historian, described his growing fascination for the "fantastic design," the "typically GDR carpets and enormous built-in cupboards," the goods lift that the porter showed them—which they repaired and put into use again—the spacious windows, the round doorknobs, and the rectangular decorations on the ceiling. Frank Peter Thomas added that all these features made him aware of the historical context in which they had been created:

> For me, the history of the building was not at first important, it was simply the place looks interesting because it still has a mosaic decoration and funny windows and is built of unusual materials, it is architecturally significant, but of course it was created because of history. Because there was a GDR, there is this mosaic, and because there was a GDR, there are these toned-down windows which the Palast der Republik also has. [. . .] And so the history of the GDR slowly came to light. Not much was left in the building itself, but it was still evident: there was a canteen and certain functions that would never have been incorporated under a capitalist regime, communal rooms, conference rooms. Of course, every hotel has conference rooms these days, but not in the dimensions of those built in the GDR period. It didn't have to be that efficient, but it was important that the management be controlled somehow (Figure 7).

The relationship that developed between the incoming tenants and the history of the buildings was an interaction. On the one hand, the architecture influenced people's work and the social relationships inside the building. Several individuals told me that the interior layout of the Haus des Lehrers provided exceptional conditions for an intensive social interaction. All the offices were located around a large corridor, where people came into contact and presented their work to each other. This gave rise to many exchanges and cooperations between people with various professional backgrounds; it was an exceptional, dynamic, and cross-fertilizing atmosphere. The architecture influenced the social relationships between the participants, but did not determine their behavior. On the other hand, people were inspired by the architecture and transformed it into something new. Rob Savelberg even said that the new users of the Haus des Lehrers brought the building back to life:

Figure 7
The Haus des Lehrers with its toned-down windows.

It was GDR, it stank of musty carpets, musty cupboards, and musty telephone lines. Everything was musty. The first thing we did was to bring our synthesizers, our computers and all our materials inside, we tore out the carpet, cut off the curtains, opened the windows wide, and brought the building back to life. It had passed away.

New tenants accepted a direct confrontation with the building and its history; they did not deny it, but they started an interaction with the traces from a recent past: "In fact, we were seduced by the charm of the GDR architecture to occupy a building from the Sixties in the postmodern Nineties and to appreciate it—and we cultivated that for the outside world." The same is true of the WMF-Club, where GDR inner architecture was recovered to be resuscitated, recycled, and transformed into something new. These various examples show that if newcomers were unaware of the historic and symbolic meaning of the buildings into which they moved, they soon developed a consciousness for these aspects, which even contributed to a positive valuation of this architecture. Several people said: "We all thought it was cool to work in a GDR atmosphere."

The appropriation of undesired architecture by new users is related to their perception of the buildings and their historic background. In a book entitled *Die Erinnerung an "das Herz der Stadt." Geschichts- und Gedächtnisbilder vom Potsdamerplatz* (1991), Dieteke van der Ree has taken the Potsdamerplatz in Berlin as her research subject for studying the perception of the built environment in the recollection of certain events. She uses the work of Pierre Nora to define two kinds of remembrance: "images from memory" and "images from history." She then compares these two types of remembrance with two kinds of observation: "images at eye level" and "images at a distance." If certain episodes are lacking in someone's experience (if the person lived somewhere else at that time or was simply not yet born) or if someone's observations are influenced by a professional background (like an architect, planner or journalist), then the person will have—for the most part—"images at a distance" in mind, for example maps, cards or clichés. These images are often expressed in metaphors or in other symbolic terms. Applying van der Ree's remarks to the present case, we could say that the general, negative perception of the Plattenbauten and other GDR architecture is based on "images at a distance" and lacks an awareness of the specificity of the buildings themselves. As "images at a distance" very often represent the perception of professionals, they do not always have to be negatively biased: in another context, politicians could have an interest in preserving certain buildings, or investors could see a gap in the market.

When people have personally experienced an event, they have observed it "at eye level;" they remember it as "images from memory" (sometimes fragmented), and they also describe it as such. These images are rich in personal experiences, but the people are rarely able to objectify or contextualize the buildings. In the present case, the perception of the original tenants is mainly constituted of "images at eye level." My emphasis has mainly been on positive valuations, but high vacancy rates in non-renovated apartments show that negative "images at eye level" can also exist and lead hundreds of thousands of people to move out. Finally, most newcomers refused the predominantly negative "images at a distance," but they could not fall back on "images at eye level," because they had not experienced this architecture before German reunification. Their images are of a third kind, which I would call "images from within." As I argued before, incoming tenants firstly and primarily experience the buildings from within; the experience of their inner space and functionality gives them access to the history from which the architecture has emerged. The movement from "images at a distance," via "images at eye level," to "images from within" follows Allen Carlson's "path of appreciation:" from a very distant perception of GDR architecture, first almost "flying over it," approaching it, then coming closer and circling around it, and finally entering it. Just as the generalizing, stereotyping "images at a distance" lack an awareness of the specificity of the buildings in themselves, so the "images from within" tend to portray the buildings as disconnected from their context. Most "images from within" are, in this case, very positive, but they could also fade away if other buildings become more hip.

These notions constitute a simplified presentation of a dynamic situation, and people can switch from one kind of perception to another. For example, the newcomers' detached approach to their homes theoretically allows a large public to share in their experience, both people with "images at a distance" and people with "images at eye level." Nevertheless, the historic awareness to which an experience of the buildings from within possibly gives rise can also become opposed to the detachment described before, which is a fundamental condition for the commoditization of GDR architecture. This is what happened to the Haus des Lehrers in the eyes of many newcomers as they became increasingly aware of the architectural, historic, and symbolic value of the building, especially when in 2001, a developer expressed his wish to acquire the building. He proposed to preserve the mosaic on the facade as dictated by the Office of Listed Buildings, but the entire inner architecture that made the building so characteristic of the period in which it was built would be replaced by a standard office interior. Rob Savelberg, who had an office in the Haus des Lehrers at that time, used strip lights to build letters behind the windows of the ninth floor which, when illuminated at night, formed the words "Not for sale" as a clear protest against the plans of the developer. Savelberg enumerated once more all the special characteristics of the building: its fantastic design and furniture, its fascinating history, its exceptional location on the "only real and authentic centre of Berlin, the Alexanderplatz," "the experimental garden of Europe". After two years in the Haus des Lehrers, Savelberg's message in the press was:

> In the name of a supposed profit maximisation and redevelopment a proven incubator will be destroyed. Second, the location Alexanderplatz 4 is worth more than the sale tag of DM 20 million. Third, in Berlin already over 9% of offices are empty, i.e. hundreds of thousands of square meters of expensive space. Throughout the city there are English FOR SALE signs or simply SALE! signs posted everywhere. The sale to this investor is a

sell out, and we the society of tenants are NOT FOR SALE. These investors do not dare and cannot buy us, buy us up or buy us out. The house and its inhabitants are unsaleable.

Savelberg's project was very expressive but it did not have any influence on city planning matters; users of the Haus des Lehrers were powerless to do anything about the sale.[19] The project did not even receive as much attention in the media as earlier projects did. People had moved in for the functional qualities of the architecture and the relatively low rent, but very quickly they had become fascinated by the uniqueness of the place and started to see it as something very special or even "uncommon, incomparable, unique, singular, and therefore not exchangeable for anything else" (Kopytoff 1986: 69). Perhaps this could explain why NOT FOR SALE was not as efficient as previous projects. When the developer expressed his intention to buy it, Savelberg and other tenants tried to present it as a "non-commodity," i.e. as something "'priceless' in the full sense of the term, ranging from the uniquely valuable to the uniquely worthless" (p. 75). Tenants had become attached to the building, but it was precisely their unbiased perspective, their detachment, which initially allowed them to approach it as an object in itself and gave their approach an exceptional strength. When they started to emphasize the singularity of the building, they began to argue on the same level as the people with "a right to inhabit the dominant image of the city"—but in these discussions they were clearly lacking economic and political power and support. As Kopytoff has emphasized:

> Behind the extraordinary vehement assertions of aesthetic values may stand conflicts of culture, class, and ethnic identity, and the struggle over the power of what one might label the "public institutions of singularization." [. . .] Power often asserts itself symbolically precisely by insisting on its right to singularize an object, or a set or class of objects (Kopytoff 1986: 73, 81).

In this situation, the new tenants clearly did not have and could not acquire "the right to singularize" the Haus des Lehrers.

CULTURALLY GENTRIFIED EYESORES

Now that both positive and negative perceptions of GDR architecture have been analyzed, the question may be posed again, what did the newcomers' perspectives on GDR architecture contribute to the debates? Did the new images that they created permanently alter the predominantly negative perception of these buildings?

In a sociological study for Humboldt University, Awuku *et al.* (2001) asked if the new popularity of Plattenbauten should be interpreted as a trend or if it consists of a series of individual interests that do not form a collective movement. The scope of their research was too narrow to draw definitive conclusions, but the authors had the feeling that the growing popularity was not as striking as the coverage in the media would suggest. The friends and acquaintances of incoming tenants reacted positively to their new apartments but did not imitate them—a necessary condition for the development of a trend. In addition, a direct experience of the Plattenbauten from within seemed to be a necessary condition for significant changes in perception to occur—attractive images in the media are insufficient to provoke these changes (Awuku *et al.* 2001: 17–18).

My respondents indicated that there is a large interest in GDR architecture—the WMF-Club, for example, is very popular. Similarly, in the Summer of 2002, three students from the Kunsthochschule Weißensee organized an interdisciplinary project entitled *Dostoprimetschatjelnosti* (Russian for "objects or places of interest") in an empty Plattenbau in Hellersdorf. Fifty artists from all over the world lived and worked there for two months. Presentations, exhibitions and parties attracted hundreds of people. Perhaps it is "easier" to display interest in the so-called DDR-Sonderbauten than in the Plattenbauten because the private sphere is not concerned. Nevertheless, several Plattenbauten residents told me that friends had reacted very positively to their new homes and could even imagine making the same choice. Frank Peter Thomas recalled:

> Our acquaintances at first took pity on us: "Oh, you have to live in a high-rise and it's a Plattenbau. Do you really like it?" We reply: "Yes, it's great." They all had very funny reservations and prejudices about the house. People only know the Leipzigerstrasse from driving fast through it. Then we had a party, and the effect was really impressive: everyone was delighted and felt that we had a very beautiful flat. That removed a bit of the shock. Everyone who had come to the party have said since then: "It's beautiful," and many asserted that they would also like to live in such a house.

Whether the new users of GDR architecture can be defined as one specific group or not, and whether it is possible to speak about a trend or not, it is clear that this architecture, despite its generally negative reputation, received much attention in the media and gained a new popularity for a significant number of people.

The arrival of newcomers, taking over some of the Plattenbauten and other former GDR buildings, appreciating them in an unexpected way and subsequently presenting them as trendy, attractive places—which then proves infectious to some of their acquaintances—all these characteristics suggest similarities to a process of gentrification. Typically, this phenomenon "involves both a change in the social composition of an area and its residents, and a change in the nature of the housing stock (tenure, price, condition, etc.)" (Hamnett 1991: 176). The concept of gentrification is interesting in this case because it emphasizes the differences, the influence and the potentials (notably due to differences in so-called "cultural capital") of the various groups involved. Nevertheless, the social changes that Hamnett mentions are generally presented as a shift from working- to middle-class residents.[20] In addition, changes in the built infrastructure of a gentrifying district are not limited to the purely residential aspects but as Neil Smith and Peter Williams have emphasized in the introduction of their work *Gentrification of the City* (1986):

> [. . .] residential gentrification is integrally linked to the redevelopment of urban waterfronts for recreational and other functions, the decline of remaining inner-city manufacturing facilities, the rise of hotel and convention complexes and central-city office developments, as well as the emergence of modern "trendy" retail and restaurant districts (Smith and Williams 1986: 3).

Even if various authors do not emphasize exactly the same aspects in their approach to gentrification processes, these few explanatory remarks do make clear that the concept of gentrification does not apply to the case of the Plattenbauten as naturally as it may have seemed. On the one hand, the number of newcomers to the Plattenbauten is significant, their presence does contribute to the upgrading transformation of certain GDR apartment blocks, which is connected to an emerging interest in the qualities of these buildings as exemplified, notably, by the intensive renovation undertaken by certain housing corporations,[21] and all this has received extensive coverage in various media. On the other hand, the differences between the original inhabitants and newcomers cannot be described in terms of class: first, because the Plattenbauten population is traditionally—and currently— very mixed; second, because the newcomers are also more differentiated than most approaches to gentrification would suggest;[22] and third, because the most significant contrast between "old" and "new" inhabitants is between East and West. It must be added that the original inhabitants are not displaced by the newcomers; rather, they live side by side. Newspaper articles have reported about tenants who had to leave their apartments in more peripheral districts of other East German towns because high vacancy rates made it impossible to preserve the building, but many of them wanted to move into—and were granted— similar housing (Rosenkranz 2001). Certain renovated apartments near the city center have become owner-occupied property, but not to an extent that it would make the place inaccessible to the original tenants. Finally, it could be stated that some intrinsic qualities of GDR apartment blocks—too standardized, not luxurious enough, and not flexible enough to be transformed into more exclusive housing—make them unsuitable, in the long term, for further gentrification in terms of an inflation of real-estate values. Not in the least influenced by a Western perception, most potential investors continue to associate Plattenbauten with a low socioeconomic status.

Despite these remarks, I would not like to abandon the concept of gentrification, as I believe it can be very useful when approached from another perspective. The material presented up to now suggests that, although gentrification in terms of social and economic changes does not completely apply here, there is nevertheless a competition between groups of people with divergent images of the Plattenbauten over "the right to inhabit the dominant image of the city." In an article entitled "In the Pursuit of Difference: Representations of Gentrification" (1996), Lees warns about the bias of the various gentrification texts that these people produce (academic, journalist, realtor, and gentrifier) and which are, in his opinion, far from neutral, and imbued with personal interests:

> Gentrification as a site of difference is expressive of urban change, transformation, hybridity, and individuality. [. . .] the positioning of gentrification as a site of difference was intellectually, politically, and economically strategic: by academics who were hoping to open up a new urban literature; by journalists (media) who were attempting to illustrate a story, to emphasize something new in city living; by realtors, who used difference in their niche marketing to attract buyers and renters into inner-city neighbourhoods; and by gentrifiers themselves, in a narcissistic run for individuality (Lees 1996: 455–6).

In an attempt to go beyond the bias implied in these different discourses and to find out the deeper motivations of the various groups of people involved, more attention has to be paid to the cultural aspects of gentrification, as suggested by Jon Caulfield: "Often, culture is acknowledged as somehow or other part of the gentrification process, but its exact role—the role of the influence of philosophic or aesthetic values or of structures of feeling about everyday life—usually remains in a black box" (Caulfield 1989: 620). In this line of thought, what can be observed in Berlin is basically a process of cultural gentrification in the sense that newcomers, although they have not physically displaced the original tenants, tend to gentrify the latter's experience(s) and image(s) of GDR architecture.

If newcomers initially moved in for purely practical or financial reasons, they soon became aware of the potential and meaning of the architecture in which they were living and/or working. Then they started to use these buildings very consciously, either to find out or to present more possibilities, or to convey a specific message. Christian Lagé, one of the organizers of the project in Hellersdorf, told me that they explored the utmost limits of what the Plattenbau allowed them to do; the next step would have been to remove certain walls. Their investigation was visible both inside and outside the building. To launch the project, they hung an enormous banner between their own and the adjacent Plattenbau, with their website: www.anschlaege.de (German for "attacks"). This action provoked many reactions from the neighbors, who wondered if the attacks were meant literally or figuratively. Users of the Haus des Lehrers (Teachers' House) even saw themselves as a new generation of teachers, as young professionals who could teach other people their discoveries. Finally, Frank Peter Thomas and his housemate, as a provocation, made a website[23] where they severely criticized historic architecture and ironically declared the Fernsehturm (the television mast, built in GDR times on the Alexanderplatz) a guardian angel against flash ornaments and bad taste:

> Robogon opposes built trash and smeared Greek style and calls the television mast his guardian angel in the battle against the misused ornament. The dreadful sight of the highly swanking fuss at the Gendarmenmarkt will no longer lead to furrowing of brows as the television mast strengthens your neuronal resistance.

These examples show that newcomers in GDR architecture are using and, in a sense, appropriating GDR material culture and transforming its meaning. This corresponds to what Caroline Mills describes in her article "Myths and Meanings of Gentrification" (1993): "One might, then, interpret gentrification as the victory over a hegemonic urban imagery by a new symbolism coupled to an emergent cultural manifesto. However, new visions may be co-opted in the reforging of hegemonic discourse by the machinery of dominant culture" (Mills 1993: 151). Plattenbauten inhabitants thus have to face more than the generally negative perception of their place of residence in the media and the stigmatizing association with criminality, anonymity and right-wing radicalism. They also perceive how newcomers—West Berliners, West Germans, Western Europeans—with a positive appreciation of Plattenbauten are appropriating traces of their recent history in which part of their identity is rooted. The meanings that newcomers attribute to GDR architecture are not only related to taste, but also to a new appreciation or even a rewriting of GDR history. The term "Ostalgie" (nostalgia for the East) has become very common to refer to a growing interest in and appeal emanating from GDR material culture, which can be illustrated by the revival of GDR design, the enormous success of the film *Goodbye, Lenin*, exhibitions such as *Kunst in der DDR* (*Art in the GDR*) in the Berliner Nationalgalerie, the creation of a Plattenbauten Museum in Dresden, the organization of numerous cultural projects in empty Plattenbauten,[24] etc. Very symptomatic for the (re-)writing of GDR history that parallels the more entertaining part of this revival is the production of GDR souvenirs, such as "System 80/25" produced by Superclub Berlin for a large project in Halle Neustadt: these souvenirs consist of two original wall plugs fixed together back to back like a photo frame, displaying a small piece of authentic GDR wallpaper (Figure 8). They are presented in very fashionable boxes with a stamp in GDR fonts, reproducing the numbers of the wall plugs, referring to their precise location in a specific room of a specific apartment in a specific building.

However, this so-called nostalgia for the East is a much more complex phenomenon than the relative superficiality of commercialization and entertainment incentives might suggest. Indeed, as Paul Betts has analyzed in his article "The Twilight of the Idols: East German Memory and Material Culture" (2000): "[. . .] ex-GDR consumer objects [. . .] have emerged as new historical markers of socialist experience and identity. [. . .] Where GDR goods once served as a source of perennial dissatisfaction and embarrassment, they later became emblems of pride and nostalgia" (Betts 2000: 734, 741). The meanings that newcomers are projecting on GDR architecture are not necessarily in line with how the original tenants identify with these concrete embodiments of their recent past. Firstly, Betts writes that the memories attached to GDR material culture are of a fundamentally collective character: "While markers of social distinction long existed within this allegedly classless society [. . .] the memories of GDR material culture have tended to reinforce, not undermine, East German solidarity" (p. 754). Here we may notice a significant difference with the circulation of images produced by the newcomers, who emphasize a very individualistic way of living and a concept of home as a means of self-construction and self-presentation. Secondly, "the importance of housing, architecture, and city planning as the preferred sites of socialist cultural identity [has] markedly shifted toward commodities and domestic spaces by the late 1950" (p. 758). This also applies to the post-1989 nostalgia, which has primarily focused on everyday consumer objects. The fact that these objects matter so much for former GDR citizens in terms of cultural identification partly explains why some of them resist the image making of the newcomers who also focus on the inside of the Plattenbauten—decoration styles, arrangement of furniture, unique objects—and are, in that sense, appropriating their cultural roots. And thirdly: "Casting East German culture as fundamentally pre- or antimodern became a favorite West German parlor game after 1989" (p. 739). The perception offered by the newcomers is not entirely disconnected from this tendency: progressive, avant-garde young people come to live in the Plattenbauten, remove some of the old furniture, create minimalistic interiors with modern design, and "bring the building back to life," as Rob Savelberg mentioned with regard to the Haus des Lehrers. Does this not suggest that the Plattenbauten in their original state were old-fashioned and needed a trendy face-lift?

The intensive projection of meanings onto GDR material culture, in particular architecture, alarms not only the original tenants, but also those who "have a right to inhabit the dominant image of the city" and fear the consequences of a positive revaluation. Gerriet Schulz told me

Figure 8
System 80/25, a GDR souvenir produced by Superclub Berlin.

that he and others, such as the Urban Catalysts,[25] have developed ideas for a temporary use of the Palast der Republik, which is scheduled for demolition in three years' time to make way for a reconstruction of the Stadtschloß. They proposed using the place in the meantime for performances, presentations, and parties. Most responsible persons are clearly in favor of these plans, but the State, which owns the building, fears that a too-positive revaluation could endanger the plans to eliminate the palace: "Of course they are worried that when we go in there and are successful and open it up that people will see, 'Hey, it's not really that bad' and in three years everyone will say: 'We don't want to tear down the Palace.'" Jon Caulfield commented with regard to modern property entrepreneurs, that: "Like the rest of the culture industry, they cannot invent the desires they commodify but need to extract them from living culture" (Caulfield 1989: 626). In the same way, for the State and other participants in this process who mainly view GDR architecture in terms of "images at a distance," it is very difficult to control or influence what Caulfield calls "living culture," here: the newcomers' creation, circulation, and diffusion of "images from within"—this explains their fears.

CONCLUSION

The analysis of different perceptions of the Plattenbauten illustrates the relevance of alternative attitudes towards rejected architecture. Newcomers approached the buildings from within, they experienced their inner architecture and functional qualities. This was the best way to go beyond stereotypes, which are usually based on a perception from the outside and at a distance. The detached attitude that allowed such an unbiased exploration of the buildings was also a necessary condition for their mediatizing and merchandizing. The strength of alternative images is best illustrated by the fact that people who do have the power over such matters start to fear the arrival of newcomers, as with regard to the temporary use of the Palast der Republik.

Nevertheless, the experience of GDR architecture from within also made new users aware of its history. The fascination and singularization to which this could give rise may then reduce the previously displayed detachment and relativize the strength of the positive images against their negative counterparts. This is intimately connected with what Kopytoff calls "the power of [. . .] the 'public institutions of singularization.'" As was illustrated by the Haus des Lehrers, the new tenants had no chance to succeed on this level of argumentation; they were powerless to do anything about the sale.

This analysis further shows that various positive attitudes towards rejected architecture can exist simultaneously, without ever intermingling. The newcomers' relationship to the Plattenbauten differs from that of the original tenants in more than one way. Their respective conceptions of private and public space are entirely opposite: whereas domestic space had acquired a very special meaning during several decades of GDR, the newcomers have blurred the fundamental border between private and public by mediatizing the Plattenbauten interiors. Further, they display divergent home cultures and do not share the same ideas with regard to the saleability of homes. This has much to do with their respective relationships to the history from which the Plattenbauten emerged. Finally, I would like to add that, although the newcomers' presence in the Plattenbauten has received much media attention and thus found a place in the collective imagination related to these buildings, the attitude of the new tenants was always very individualistic. Despite their interest in GDR history—which they seem to perceive as something rather "peculiar"—their main motivations were to discover the Plattenbauten by themselves and to comment from their own point of view. They never primarily intended to stimulate a collective valuation of the Plattenbauten with which both the original and the new tenants would identify. Rather, they would use the material traces of this history to present themselves. In that sense, they unmistakably displayed a "narcissistic run for individuality" which, according to Lees (1996), is characteristic for gentrifiers.

In general, it is very difficult to foresee the impact of alternative attitudes towards rejected architecture, as it depends on a complex interaction between images "at a distance," "at eye level" and "from within"—implying different observations, experiences, appreciations, and attitudes towards the buildings. It also depends on whether the competing images are of the same kind or not, and whether those partaking in the debates have "the right to inhabit the dominant image of the city" or not. This shows that, apart from demolition, transformation, and acquisition, there are alternative, complex means of appropriating other people's architecture.

ACKNOWLEDGMENT

Research funding for this article was made possible by the Netherlands Organization for Scientific Research (NWO). Thanks also go to the participants in the 9th Interdisciplinary Conference on Material Culture and Consumption (June 27–9 2003, Department of Design History and Material Culture, Univeristy of Applied Arts, Vienna) and the two *Home Cultures* readers for their constructive criticism.

NOTES

1. See Geisel (2002), Steglich (1998) and Zohlen (1999).
2. All translations by the author.
3. See *Bildzeitung* (2001) Du Bois (2002) and Wewer (2001).
4. See my paper entitled "13th May 2001, 8:01 AM – 1 Building, 20 000 People and 450 Kilos of Explosives. The Explosion of Corrupt Architecture as a Secular Sacrifice."
5. See also Miller (1998: 11).
6. See, for example Finger (2003); Rosenkranz (2001).

7. All quotes by Erik Schmidt, Axel Watzke, Ulli Uphaus, Frank Peter Thomas, Gerd Wessel, Rob Savelberg, Gerriet Schulz, and Christian Lagé from interviews held July 5–8 2001 or May 4–9 2003.

8. I will nevertheless continue to use the term *Plattenbau*, because it was used by the people I spoke with: the newcomers in these prefabricated apartment blocks, who are the subject of this article. Besides that, the term simply refers to a type of building, characterized by a specific construction method using prefabricated plates.

9. See Geisel (2002: 29) and Steglich (1998).

10. "The 'view from Kienberg' is a classic of a sentimental distance, which does not want to belong to reality and discover the fear of continuously changing other places. It takes up the same position as the town planner at the drawing board, when he commits houses to designs on paper, abstract, like a helicopter pilot who can only view reality as an ornament; the inevitable fate of an architect or, in the specialist terminology of the GDR, project manager work" (Zohlen 1999: 138).

11. In a collection of articles about *Socialist Spaces: Sites of Everyday Life in the Eastern Bloc* (2002), David Crowley writes that Warsaw interiors in the 1950s and 1960s were "private sanctuaries"—not so much that they would set the stage for dissident meetings, but in a much broader sense: In the "Soviet-styled city," where "space was subordinate to images and effects, and, by the same system, interiors were inferior to the exterior forms that produced them" (Crowley 2002: 185), people would understand the private realm as "the limit of intrusions from the public sphere." This means "the home was claimed as a sanctuary, private in the sense of being a hidden or inaccessible realm" (p. 187). In the same book, Katerina Gerasimova describes the increased importance of a "symbolic privatization of domestic space" (Gerasimova 2002: 210) in the Soviet Union in the 1960s, as a reaction on several decades of openness of the private sphere to the State and the collective.

12. Penko Stoitchev, a "sound artist" who created the Ambient Lounge on the fifth floor of the Haus des Lehrers, emphasized the urban experience one step further. The place was conceived as an observatory where people could relax and enjoy the view in two directions, completed by a sound installation made of noises that were gathered in the nearby surroundings. Another project in which the Haus des Lehrers specifically acted as an observatory is *Herr Doeblin's Lounge*, by Rob Savelberg, in November 2000. It was conceived as an "after-work event." People lay on mattresses while listening to an actor reading Alfred Döblin's famous book *Berlin Alexanderplatz*. They could observe the square by night through a telescope.

13. See *Esquire* June 2001: 48–51.

14. *Homestory. A Glimpse of a Modern Artist's Living*, initially written in 1998, was published in 2002 in the catalog to the touring exhibition *Come-in. Interior Design as a Contemporary Art Medium in Germany*, commissioned by the Institut für Auslandsbeziehungen (Institute for International Relations). See http://www.ifa.de/a/ a1/come-in/dweidner.

15. See Esser (2001), Wewer (2001), Roth (2002) and Koelbl (2001).

16. See also Humphrey (2002: 185–7).

17. The WMF-Club has led a nomadic existence since the early 1990s, moving from one empty building to the next. The search for empty, affordable space soon led the initiators into GDR architecture, such as the *Ahornblatt*, a very striking, shell-shaped, concrete building that was used in GDR times as a canteen, or Café Moskau, one of the catering establishments representing the other Eastern-bloc states, where the WMF-Club recently took up residence.

18. Another example in the same building is the telephone exchange from GDR times, an enormous installation. Rob Savelberg told me that one person was responsible for making the connections. On this occasion, he was also tapping the phone calls, like he had always done before 1989. Most incoming tenants found it funny; Rob Savelberg said it gave him the feeling of living in a kind of museum or fairyland. This was of course not the same perception as people who had actually lived in the GDR.

19. After the Haus des Lehrers had been sold, certain people started privileging their individual interests in the search for a new office, and what had by that time become like a community soon fell apart. Here we see a shift from "images from within" to "images at a distance," and a very pragmatic search for other, affordable offices. Others, who absolutely wanted to stay on the Alexanderplatz, moved into the Haus des Reisens (another GDR building with a contemporary interior), and still others rented a floor in the main building of the communist newspaper *Neues Deutschland*.

20. "Gentrification [. . .] refers to the rehabilitation of working-class and derelict housing and the consequent transformation of an area into a middle-class neighbourhood" (Smith and Williams 1986: 1).

21. For example, several apartments blocks on the Platz der Vereinten Nationen (where the artist Erik Schmidt lives) were extensively renovated in 1995–6 and subsequently became listed buildings. This has been documented in an article by Gerold Perler (1998). As I mentioned before, attempts at upgrading the housing stock in Hellersdorf were also made. In general, since 1990, many property developers have asked themselves how to develop this enormous quantity of GDR housing.

22. A large majority of newcomers consists of creative workers (artists, architects, designers, advertising managers), but in an article entitled "Gentrification and Desire" (1989), Jon Caulfield has argued on the diversity of gentrifiers in terms of visibility and tenure,

occupation and income, political outlook, cultural affiliation, as well as household composition and lifestyle (Caulfield 1989: 618). His remarks also apply to the newcomers in the Plattenbauten who do not, as such, form a group, class or movement.

23. See: http://www.robogon.de.
24. Besides "Dostoprimetschatjelnosti" in Hellersdorf, for example, an empty Plattenbau in Halle-Neustadt was transformed into a hotel for several weeks in September 2003, attracting hundreds of visitors every day (see www.hotel-neustadt.de). In the same period, thirty artists were participating in a project in Hoyerswerda entitled "Superumbau—die verkunstete Platte," documenting, analyzing, and challenging the changing meanings of Plattenbauten in various cities (see www.spirit-of-zuse.de).
25. See http://www.urbancatalysts.de.

REFERENCES

Awuku, Kwadwo et al. 2001. *Die Wiederinwertsetzung der "Platte."* Projektseminar Großwohnsiedlung Ost, Humboldt Universität Berlin, Institut für Sozialwissenschaften (unpublished).

Barthes, Roland. 1997 [1964]. "The Eiffel Tower." In Neil Leach (ed.) *Rethinking Architecture: A Reader in Cultural Theory*, pp. 172–80. London: Routledge.

Betts, Paul. 2000. "The Twilight of the Idols. East German Memory and Material Culture." In *Journal of Modern History* 72: 731–65.

Bildzeitung. 2001. "Honis Platte ist wieder hipp." *Bildzeitung* June 8 2001.

Buchli, Victor. 2000. *An Archaeology of Socialism*. Oxford: Berg.

Carlson, Allen. 1994. "Existence, Location and Function: The Appreciation of Architecture." In Michael H. Mitias (ed.) *Philosophy and Architecture*, pp. 141–64. Amsterdam: Rodopi.

Caulfield, Jon. 1989. "'Gentrification' and Desire." *Canadian Review of Sociology and Anthropology* 26(4): 617–32.

Crowley, David. 2002. "Warsaw Interiors. The Public Life of Private Spaces, 1949–65." In David Crowley (ed.) *Socialist Spaces. Sites of Everyday Life in the Eastern Bloc*, Oxford: Berg.

Dörhöfer, Kerstin (ed.). 1994. *Wohnkultur und Plattenbau. Beispiele aus Berlin und Budapest*. Berlin: Reimer.

Douglas, Mary. 1996. *Thought Styles: Critical Essays on Good Taste*. London, Thousand Oaks, CA and New Delhi: Sage.

Du Bois, Pierre. 2002. "Wohnen in der Platte ist einfach kultig." *C6 Online Magazin* March 3 2002.

Esser, Christian. 2001. "Platte putzen." *Max* 12: 110–13.

Finger, Evelyn. 2003. "Rückbau Ost." *Die Zeit* July 7 2003: 49.

Geisel, Sieglinde. 2002. "Die andere Platte. Zu Besuch in Hellersdorf, DDR-Baukasten und Schmuckkästchen Ostberlins." *Foyer—Journal für Stadtentwicklung* April: 29–33.

Gerasimova, Katerina. 2002. "Public Privacy in the Soviet Communal zApartment." David Crowley (ed.) *Socialist Spaces. Sites of Everyday Life in the Eastern Bloc.* Oxford: Berg.

Hain, Simone. 2003. "The utopian potential of Plattenbau." *Dostoprimet-schatjelnosti*. Hamburg: Junius Verlag.

Hamnett, Chris. 1991. "The Blind Men and the Elephant. The Explanation of Gentrification." *Transactions of the Institute of British Geographers* 16(2): 173–89.

Humphrey, Caroline. 2002. *The Unmaking of Soviet Life. Everyday Economies after Socialism*. Ithaca, NY: Cornell University Press.

Kil, Wolfgang. 1999. "Eine Stadt wie jede andere." *Freitag—Die Ost-West Wochenzeitung* March 12 1999.

Koelbl, Susanne. 2001. "Dufte urban." *Der Spiegel* 23: 58–9.

Kopytoff, Igor. 1986. "The Cultural Biography of Things: Commoditization as Process." Arjun Appadurai (ed.) *The Social Life of Things. Commodities in Cultural Perspective*, pp. 64–91. Cambridge: Cambridge University Press.

Lees, L. 1996. "In the Pursuit of Difference: Representations of Gentrification." *Environment and Planning A* 28: 453–70.

Lüdtke, Insa Kristina. 2002. "Homestories: Eine Inszenierung zwischen Kunst und Kommerz." *Deutsche Bauzeitung* 10: 60–3.

Miller, Daniel (ed.). 1998. *Material Cultures. Why Some Things Matter*. Chicago, IL: University of Chicago Press.

——. 2001. *Home Possessions. Material Culture behind Closed Doors*. Oxford: Berg.

Mills, Caroline. 1993. "Myths and meanings of gentrification." In James Duncan and David Ley (eds) *Place/Culture/Representation*, pp. 149–70. London & New York: Routledge.

Perler, Gerold. 1998. "Fassadengestaltung am Plattenbau. Das Beispiel Platz der Vereinten Nationen in Berlin." In Holger Barth (ed.) *Projekt Sozialistische Stadt. Beiträge zur Bau- und Planungsgeschichte der DDR*. Berlin: Dietrich Reimer Verlag.

Rietdorf, Werner. 1997. "Genesis, Status und Perspektive ostdeutscher Großsiedlungen." In *Weiter wohnen in der Platte. Probleme der Weiterentwicklung großer Neubauwohngebiete in den neuen Bundesländern*, pp. 11–57. Berlin: Edition Sigma.

Rosenkranz, Jan. 2001. "Einmal Silberhöhe und zurück." *Freitag—Die Ost-West Wochenzeitung* April 11 2001.

Roth, Alisa. 2002. "In Chic New Berlin, Ugly is Way Cool." *The New York Times* January 24 2002: F1–8.

Schmidt, Erik and Corinna Weidner. 2002. "Homestory. A Glimpse of a Modern Artist's Living." In Institut für Auslandsbeziehungen (ed.) *Come-in. Interior Design as a Contemporary Art Medium in Germany*. Bonn: VG Bild-Kunst.

Schneider, Rolf. 1999. "Passagen. Notate." In Ulrich Domröse and Jack Gelfort (eds) *Peripherie als Ort. Das Hellersdorf Projekt*, pp. 93–108. Stuttgart: Arnoldsche.

Smith, Neil and Peter Williams (eds). 1986. *Gentrification of the City.* London: Allen & Unwin.

Steglich, Ulrike. 1998. "Die Rehabilitierung der Platte." *Scheinschlag* 4.

van der Ree, Dieteke. 1991. *Die Erinnerung an "das Herz der Stadt." Geschichts- und Gedächtnisbilder vom Postdamer Platz.* Amsterdam: Het Spinhuis.

Wewer, Antje. 2001. "Neues Leben in der (k)alten Platte." *Home* March 2001: 22–47.

Zohlen, Gerwin. 1999. "Die Beatmete. Gedanken zur Tradition der Großsiedlungen." In Ulrich Domröse and Jack Gelfort (eds) *Peripherie als Ort. Das Hellersdorf Projekt*, pp. 137–55. Stuttgart: Arnoldsche.

Zukin, Sharon. 1996. "Space and Symbols in an Age of Decline." In Anthony D. King (ed.) *Re-presenting the City: Ethnicity, Capital and Culture in the 21st Century Metropolis*, pp. 43–59. London: Macmillan Press.

HOME CULTURES   VOLUME 1, ISSUE 2.   REPRINTS AVAILABLE   PHOTOCOPYING   © BERG 2004
PP 127–146   DIRECTLY FROM THE   PERMITTED BY LICENSE   PRINTED IN THE UK
PUBLISHERS.   ONLY

REBECCA GINSBURG

NATIVE DAUGHTER: HOME, SEGREGATION, AND MENTAL MAPS

REBECCA GINSBURG RECEIVED HER PHD IN ARCHITECTURAL HISTORY FROM THE UNIVERSITY OF CALIFORNIA AT BERKELEY IN 2001 AND IS CURRENTLY A POSTDOCTORAL FELLOW AT WASHINGTON UNIVERSITY, ST LOUIS, WHERE SHE IS COMPLETING A MANUSCRIPT ON THE CULTURAL LANDSCAPES OF APARTHEID.

Narrow mental maps, those that present a blinkered, overly simplified view of reality, are believed to play a role in the development of prejudicial attitudes and behaviors. But what about when such maps happen to be held by members of disadvantaged groups? This paper examines the mental map of "home" held by an African-American girl who lived in a racially segregated community outside Chicago during the Depression. It finds that her map was not a simple, single construct, but consisted of overlapping, interpenetrating landscapes of sights, sounds, places, and feelings. Perhaps surprisingly, while her map was detailed and complete, it did not acknowledge the segregated nature of her family's neighborhood. The article suggests that her map served a defensive purpose, protecting her from the indignities of being a conscious victim of discrimination. It concludes that while narrow maps might indeed feed the prejudices of members of dominant groups, they may operate as instruments of empowerment among the oppressed.

One way of thinking about the divisible nature of households is to consider that the members of any given household will inevitably create and inhabit distinct domestic landscapes. The view from the master bedroom is literally and metaphorically different than that from the playroom or the kitchen. Depending on their respective interests, values, roles, physical sizes, and so on, each household resident composes her or his own mental map.[1] In any given home, we can expect no two to be the same, and for each to be telling of the place, power, and capacities of the person who holds it.

This picture is further complicated by the fact that a person's mental map or landscape is not a single, unitary, unchanging construct, but a multi-layered and fragmented thing consisting of misapprehensions from the past not yet fully discredited, and glimmerings of new perspectives and understandings. There are also various scales superimposed on one another, with "blind spots" and empty fields both acknowledged and not fully recognized.

Individuals form mental maps in the process of imposing imaginative order upon their surroundings. I turned to them to solve a puzzle that arose in the course of conducting a series of interviews about an informant's childhood home in a segregated American neighborhood during the Depression. My initial interest had been in the domestic life and material culture of a working-class African-American family, a population little dealt with during this otherwise much-studied period in American housing history.[2] However, I found myself struck as well by how my informant, also my mother, appeared to have ordered her childhood environment.[3] This is why.

My mother, Dorothy Rousseau, was born in 1925 in Morgan Park, Illinois, a neighborhood about fourteen miles south of Chicago's Loop. In Morgan Park at that time, as in many contemporary communities, an "Improvement Association" (the MPIA) and other white civic groups fought to maintain residential and educational segregation. They had considerable success, restricting black residence to a wedge-shaped district that lay between the two railway tracks (Figure 1) (Chicago Plan Commission 1942; Homel 1984: 152–3). Dorothy lived in that area of small, one-story developers' houses with her parents, three older brothers, and two sisters, just two blocks from the unofficial border that separated black and white Morgan Park. However, she knew nothing of its existence. In fact, she remained ignorant of the MPIA and the battles over local segregation that occurred throughout her childhood (see Homel 1984: 42–4, 152–7). Even more intriguingly, she did not even know that whites lived in Morgan Park.[4]

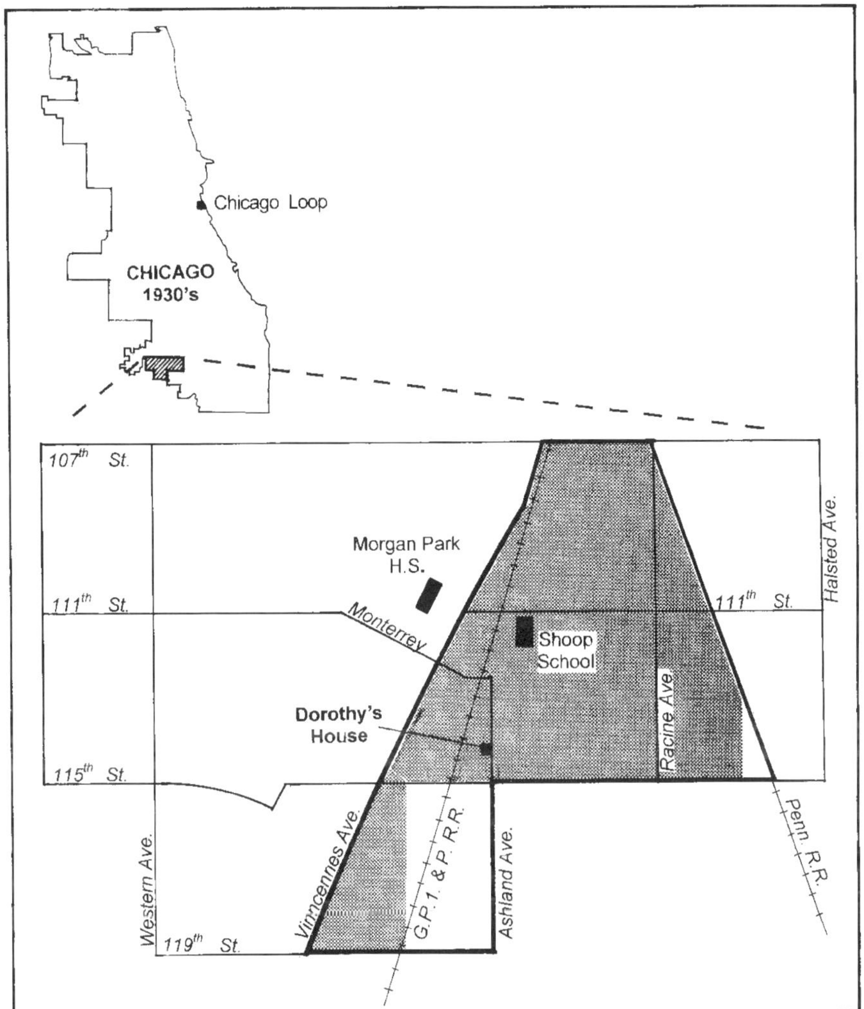

So what did she believe? According to her, Morgan Park was a small, predominantly black town that happened to be surrounded by wealthy white ones.

I take my mother's reading of her environment as an example of "naturalizing"—that is, of taking as "normal" what was in reality the result of distinct and identifiable social and historical forces. It is not difficult to understand why she did this. There is considerably greater appeal in believing that one's family lives where it does by choice or "just because" than feeling oneself to have been forced into a segregated ghetto. Nonetheless, it is challenging to imagine how a bright child could sustain such a fiction in the face of considerable evidence to the contrary. Dorothy was clever, so it was not dullness that blinded her to the reality of her social and physical environments. In addition, she

Figure 1
Map of Morgan Park, showing racial boundaries, 1930s. Shaded area shows approximate location of the district in which white residents confined black settlement in Morgan Park. Drawing: Janet Stephens.

moved widely and adventurously throughout Morgan Park and the surrounding towns, so neither was physical isolation responsible for her failure to recognize the dynamics that shaped her environment's racial geography. How could she not see what seems to have been painfully obvious, namely that her family lived where it did due to the discriminatory practices and occasional violence of neighboring whites?

It is of course impossible to reproduce exactly other people's thinking patterns, or even one's own long-discarded views. However, with enough information we can at least sketch the contours of old mental maps and identify their primary features. We can also speculate about the factors that informed them. In this article I try to piece together Dorothy's version of her childhood landscape, paying special attention to her home, as its core, and to the material and spatial elements that served as its framework. Her maps provide a good example of how such constructions can work, and possibly expand our ideas of the purposes they can serve.

> "Rat trap"—that's all it is. I remember just as well the day me and Big Walter moved in here. Hadn't been married but two weeks and wasn't planning on living here more than a year. We was going to set away, little by little, don't you know, and buy a little place out in Morgan Park.
>
> Hansberry 1958: 128, *Raisin in the Sun*

The Blue Island Land and Building Company plotted Morgan Park in the 1870s on a piece of land south of the city that included both flatland and one of the few ridges in the Chicago area. Intended as a streetcar suburb, the area was served by the Rock Island Railroad, which provided a forty-minute ride to downtown. Most of its houses were one-story, single-family homes, except on the heights where the wealthier residents built large mansions. Lots sold well, and the residents voted for incorporation in 1882. Though separated from the city by open fields and wooded areas, Morgan Park did not remain a separate town for long. Chicago annexed the approximately two and a half square mile district in 1914 (Chicago Plan Commission 1942: 76–7).[5]

Morgan Park's population was predominantly white, but from its earliest days African-Americans established households there as well. Most worked as live-out servants in local white homes (Chicago Commission on Race Relations 1922: 137). The black migration in the 'teens augmented Morgan Park's black population in two ways. First, although they were more likely to find their way to the Black Belt, the predominantly African-American neighborhood that extended from just below the Loop to about 39th Street, a few newcomers moved directly from southern states to Morgan Park.[6]

The more common pattern, though, was for longer-term, middle-class residents of the Belt to move out as the influx created increasingly stressed living conditions there. It was not simply a matter of rising numbers, though, according to US census figures, the Belt's population grew from 34,335 residents in 1910 to 92,501 in 1920, almost tripling in ten years (Chicago Commission on Race Relations 1922: 107). The greater difficulty was that organized white resistance to black residence outside the Belt's borders limited expansion of the district.[7] As a consequence, while numbers swelled, the size of the Black Belt did not. Overcrowding and lack of investment by landlords led to deteriorating housing conditions. Many residents complained also about changing standards of behavior and having to live among newly urbanized families who still practiced "country" ways. Some who could afford to moved out, heading for those few other areas that still allowed African-American occupation.[8]

These communities, inevitably more expensive than the Black Belt and hence economically restrictive, included neighborhoods in the Near North Side, Roseland in the far south, and Morgan Park (Spear 1967: 146). Its black population grew from 126 in 1910 to 695 in 1920, and had ballooned to about 5,000 by 1940.[9] Attracting mostly city-hall employees, clerks, porters, and other members of what in early-twentieth-century America constituted the black middle class, Morgan Park developed a reputation as a conservative, stable, "respectable" community. *The Report of the Chicago Commission on Race Relations* described it in 1922 as "attractive with comfortable homes and large grounds . . . The white people of Morgan Park are not unfriendly towards their Negro neighbors, though there seems to be a common understanding that Negroes must not live west of Vincennes Road" (Chicago Commission on Race Relations 1922: 137).

Anna and John Rousseau, Dorothy's parents, moved to Chicago from Arkansas some time between 1921 and 1923, after the height of the migration, but part of the same trend. Like the tens of thousands who had come before them, they fled the indignities of southern life—where you had to step off a sidewalk if a white person came along, as they often told their children. "Jim Crow" was John's shorthand way of denoting discriminatory treatment in housing, jobs, and education, and the reason he and Anna had decided to leave. They fled more personal pains as well, for in Arkansas Anna had buried her first husband and four daughters, all of whom had died of the same genetic condition before she turned twenty-five.

The search for expanded opportunities for themselves and their children that motivates most migrants was reinforced in the Rousseau's case by their image of themselves as successful go-getters. "We Rousseaus always did get up and do," Mr Rousseau often said, referring in part to his father's journey from being enslaved on a large Georgia plantation to farming his own land in Arkansas by the end of the century. For reasons that remain unclear to Dorothy, her grandfather lost his farm in the early 1900s, when John was still a teenager, but family pride in his accomplishment remained. John married Anna Dowden about ten years later. Like him, she was born and bred in Arkansas and, like him, she was ready to leave it. After the birth of their third son, they finally bid farewell to the South.

The Rousseau's first home was on 36th Street in the Belt, not far from where John's sister, Babe, had settled some years earlier. Verna, the first girl, was born there. After a couple of years, feeling the pressures of crowded city living, yearning for the green open spaces that they themselves had grown up with, and aspiring to provide for their children more of the advantages that a Pullman porter's relatively high income might afford, John and Anna moved their family to Morgan Park. They bought a brand new four-room house on the corner of 114th and Ashland, with an outdoor toilet in the back and an empty, undeveloped lot across the street.

There were four identical houses next door, probably constructed by the same developer, each wooden frame on concrete blocks, with an open porch in front and a basement. There was no running water and no electricity. The kitchen had a wood-burning stove, and they fetched water from a hydrant or "plug" on 115th Street. Even before the two youngest girls, Dorothy and Helen, were born, Mr Rousseau had begun what would become a virtual lifetime of renovation projects. "Don't have to worry about keeping up with the Joneses," he used to say. "Let the Joneses keep up with us."

He added two rooms in the back; they became a bedroom and kitchen, respectively. Then he built a wall through what had become the middle bedroom to create an indoor bathroom. He went on to enclose the front porch and add a new enclosed porch off the kitchen in back. Eventually he finished three rooms in the basement, two bedrooms and a play area (Figure 2). A 1930 insert of a fire insurance map of Chicago published by the Sanborn Map Co. in 1950 (Vol. 49) reveals the Rousseau family had the largest house on the block (Figure 3).

What did Dorothy know of this place? By now she was five, and had begun the process of deciphering her surroundings. However, rather than examine in detail the development of her map through its various stages, I want to jump ahead and study its form at a particular point in time, when she was around eleven or twelve. Children at that age can comprehend the geographical concept of "city," and by this time Dorothy seems to have acquired the understanding of Morgan Park that she would retain throughout the rest of her years there. It was 1938. World War II had not started, but she was aware of vague troubles in Europe, mostly because the Polish nuns at the Catholic school she attended spoke often and bitterly about foreign affairs. She does not remember hearing the term "Depression," probably because conditions were no worse for her family and neighbors than they had ever been. She and her sisters stuffed cardboard in their shoes and wore skirts of recycled feed sacks that they bought from neighbors who kept chickens. They sold homegrown pumpkins along the highway to white people who stopped on their way to the nearby country club, and her brothers earned extra money by returning their runaway golf balls. Her father had built

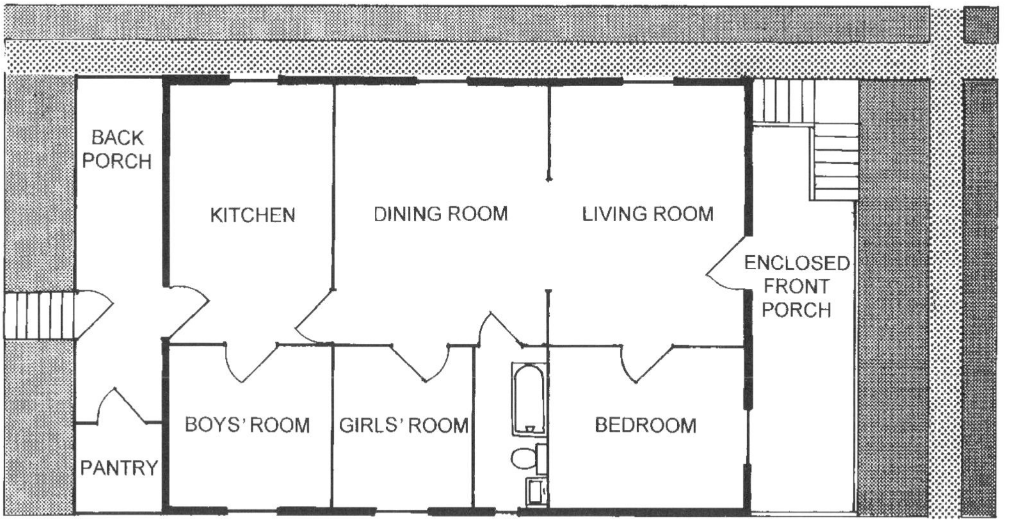

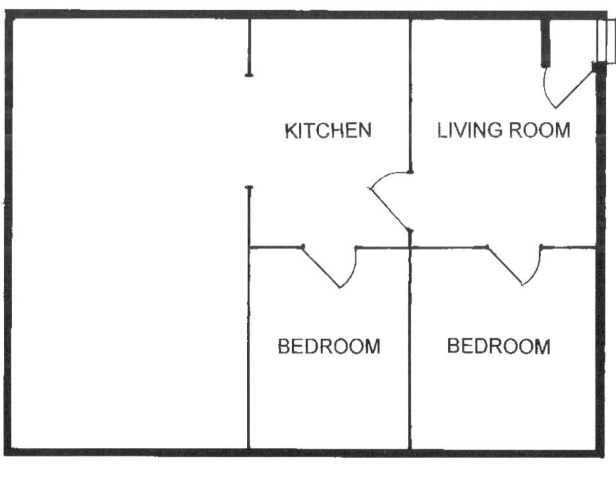

Figure 2
Plan of Rousseau house, 1938. The original house consisted of the first four rooms. John Rousseau added the kitchen, back bedroom, bathroom, and back porch by 1930. By 1938 he had also finished the basement rooms, where the boys moved, leaving Verna in the former boys' room and Dorothy and Helen alone in the girls' room. Drawing: Janet Stephens.

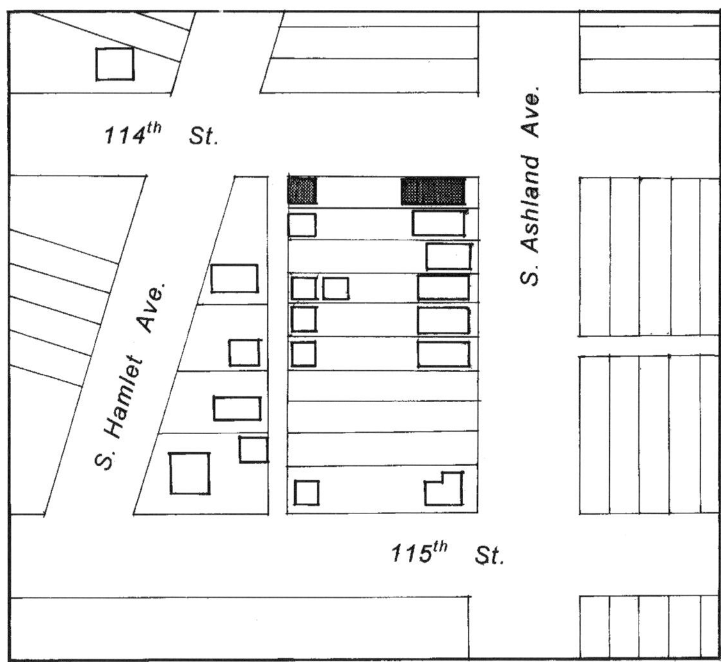

Figure 3
Sanborn fire insurance map, 1930. The Rousseau house is shaded. Drawing: Janet Stephens.

a garage by then, though her family did not own a car, and one summer a couple moved in with all their furniture and lived there until the cold weather set in. Dorothy thought it strange but, then, folks were always making room for family and friends. Boarders and houseguests were as much a fact of life as hand-me-downs and leftovers from whites' kitchens that domestics brought home and distributed to their neighbors. "We thought that whites were better than we were, but we didn't know why or how."[10]

HER MAP

The heart of Dorothy's map was her family home, but it did not register simply as a rectangular shape in a large, flat landscape. Rather, "home" consisted of various layers of interpenetrating landscapes, each composed of an assemblage of places, sounds, sights, and feelings. None existed as bird's-eye views of the territory. Rather, they were impressions and images of strong emotive content that, while they corresponded to real, physical, grounded sites, fit together into geographies of the mind that resist representation in two-dimensional form.

The space behind the bureau; private, quiet, cramped. Dorothy liked to crawl back here, in the triangular area between the bureau's back and the corner of the living room. She would sit on the floor and eat sardine cracker sandwiches and get lost in her library books or comics.

It was her secret place, though everyone knew they could find her there, and formed part of her personal landscape. Other points on this landscape included the front porch, where she and her middle brother, Biggy, sketched and drew. Sometimes she wrote love letters for Booker, a boy in her class who paid her five cents for each one. Biggy helped her with some of the language.

The space on the linoleum floor in front of the Philco radio in the living room. She and Helen ran home from school at noon so they wouldn't miss any of Ma Perkins' or Helen Trent's daily adventures. Helen Trent had a fiancé who seemed perpetually on the verge of kissing her, but frustratingly never did. Anna would set up their lunches of bologna or peanut-butter sandwiches or baked beans on chairs in front of the speaker and they sat on the floor with their ears as close as possible to it.

One of Dorothy's chores was to water the vegetable garden that the Rousseaus kept in the empty lot across the street. She loved this job. Green, fresh, wet. The wind blew and rustled the plants. The only downside was the cabbage worms, which she hated. Her cousin, Dempsey, who lived down the street with Uncle Leroy and Aunt Queen, often joined her and they had long, rambling talks. They figured out that they could lie on their stomachs in the center of the garden and fix the hose to spray straight ahead, so that they only had to rotate four times, never rising, to do the whole lot.

She did not have her own wardrobe, dresser drawer, desk, or closet, as there were no closets in the house. However, the black iron hook on the wall of the bedroom that she shared with Helen was hers. She hung her clothes there. The only seat at the dining room table that was reserved was the one at the head of the table, and that was for John, when he was in town. But she had a favorite place along one side, and she tried to grab it whenever she could. All these places—or, rather, the constellation formed by them—helped to distinguish her from her sisters, brothers, and parents, who operated within different orbits in the same rooms.

On a second level, there were things and spaces that distinguished her house from the houses around it. The immediate neighborhood seems to have been built by a single developer. She cannot remember ever entering a house that had a basic floor plan different from her own. However, there was room for variety within the details, and it was the details that were ripe with meaning.

One of Dorothy's strongest memories is of needing to use a neighbor's toilet one day and being shown to a room that had an indoor toilet—most of the houses did by the mid-1930s—but nothing else. She was so surprised that she came home and told her father. "Lots of people don't have bathtubs," he said, matter-of-factly. It was a revelation that everyone did not live more or less as she did. At that moment, the porcelain tub assumed greater importance in her mind, and she started to view see her house in a new light. Even after her neighbors began to install bathtubs of their own—and not all of them did—she remained conscious of the fact that her family was the first.

In other ways, too, she began to distinguish her house. No one had had indoor plumbing in the early days of the black migration to Morgan Park. People regularly fetched household water from the public hydrant on 115th Street. Because Ashland Avenue was a main thoroughfare, Dorothy saw them passing back and forth regularly in front of her house. Their buckets swung in the air when empty, splashed when overfull on the return trip. After the Rousseau's installed plumbing, not only did her brothers stop making trips to the plug, but so did the folks around them. The Rousseau house was closer, so neighbors came to them now, filling their buckets at the Rousseau's taps in the front and back yards. Housewives would sometimes come up the back steps to the kitchen. "Mrs. Rousseau, I'm preparing dinner. Could you just give me a cup of water, please?" If her parents objected to these practices, Dorothy could not tell, for they never complained.

The Rousseau's were the first in the neighborhood to have a telephone, too, and this brought even more neighbors to the Rousseau place. Whereas water trips typically ended at the outside taps or just inside the back door, folks on telephone business had to come right inside the Rousseau's house. No one in Morgan Park locked their doors, so grown-ups—for this was adult business only—simply walked up the Rousseau's front stairs and entered the front porch. The children were not allowed to use the front door to enter or leave the house, but adult visitors could. They gave a little knock as they hollered through the open front door that led straight into the living room. "Mr. Rousseau, Mrs. Rousseau, I'm here," they would call, before passing into the dining room, where the phone sat on a small table. Dorothy remembers her father getting annoyed when they put slugs rather than nickels into the slot.

The neat, modern house was a source of pride and identity to Dorothy and her siblings, as was her parents' reputations as neighborly, decent folks for making their technologies available for general use. Earlier memories reinforced her view of the house as an important community landmark. Years before, Anna and John had kept a small general store in the basement. They sold flour, cornmeal, sugar, and other dry goods in big bins that sat on the floor. Customers accessed the shop from the external stairs underneath the front porch. Dorothy had never worked in the store; she was too young. However, she was aware of the comings and goings of neighbors who interrupted her mother during the day to ask if the could please buy something, and understood that her home was a source of goods and resources.

There was a final item of domestic furnishing that reinforced Dorothy's sense of the uniqueness of her house and its place in the landscape. Her home was the only one she had ever seen with books. Daddy kept his "library" of twenty or thirty volumes in a wooden cabinet with glass doors that were always kept closed to protect its precious contents. There was a Bible, a dictionary, Tom Sawyer, works by Shakespeare and

Dickens, and many books about checkers, John's hobby. He turned regularly to them to improve his game, and from her father Dorothy learned that you could look up the answer to any question. Once she went to the public library and brought home three books on a single topic. She can not remember what the subject was, but she recalls that her mother hit her on the head and chided her: "Three books on the same thing?" But Dorothy knew she was right, that no two books yielded exactly the same information and that each volume represented a unique view on the world.

It was not only what her father's library represented in terms of knowledge that accounted for its hold on her, however. Its magic came in part because the source of his books was unknown. Her parents had never sold books in the basement. Mr Eldridge did not carry them in his shop on 115th, and she'd never seen them at the G & L grocery store, which carried about everything else the family needed. The public library had books, of course, but they were not for sale. Where did people get books from? Dorothy reasoned that they had something to do with trains, for often when Daddy returned on a run from New York City, his regular route, he would enter the house with a new book under his arm. The volumes disconnected her family's house from its immediate surroundings and placed it in some other sphere, tied to faraway places that were unknown and mystical.

Dorothy's map, then, contained a network of places in and around the house that constituted her personal sphere. The route from the girls' bedroom to the back of the bureau, for instance, the trail along the garden floor that had become worn by her footsteps, and the spot on the porch where she rested her back while drawing were components of this spatial system. That she was unaware of its existence on a conscious level made it no less important. This personal landscape was the platform from which she looked out and interpreted the world. It was also a source of her identity and a means of inscribing her presence in a full household.

Superimposed on this was a layer of landscape that depicted a house in relation to its immediate environment. What Dorothy composed here was the sense of a structure drawing people to it from the surrounding blocks. The comings and goings of adults to the phone and youngsters to the taps grounded the Rousseau house and gave it a metaphorically central position in the dozen or so blocks that composed her portion of Morgan Park. At the same time, the books lifted it from its moorings and placed her house in a different sphere all together. The house was like a magnet, drawing things to it, but also like an octopus that reached far and wide.

It is clear that artifacts and the stories they tell help us to situate ourselves. Spatial relationships are another sort of "thing." They can be encountered and interpreted as well, and serve as yet another source of information about ourselves. Indeed, spatial organization is a particularly strong source of information about place; it speaks explicitly to where we fit in the order of things. With this in mind, we can continue to examine Dorothy's mental maps.

As she moved further from the spots and things that constituted "home," other sites appeared on Dorothy's map. While they were clearly not family territory, their interest lay in part in what they told of the wider contexts of the Rousseau house. They thereby contributed to the construction of meaning about that place. The Roberts sisters, Baby Sis and Feet, were two of her closest friends. Dorothy sat on the steps of their front porch of their home a block down Ashland and told them stories that she made up on the spot. Their brothers told her they were Joe Louis's cousins, and she believed them until the boys down the street said the same thing.

On lazy afternoons when there was nothing else to do, she and her siblings would go to Mr Bishop's funeral parlor to see who was recently dead and try to steal flowers from the arrangements. Around the corner on 114th, her best friend, Doris Martin, lived. She and Helen shared their three dolls, Molly, Polly, and Dolly with her. Doris's mother worked in white people's houses all year long, the only full-time working mother among Dorothy's friends. Dorothy often saw her coming home at the end of the day carrying bags full of things her employers had given her.

The intersection on 115th Street and Ashland had associations of another sort. It seemed that every weekend there was an accident there, mostly involving white people heading down to the country club or the race track. Dorothy and the other Rousseau children went to watch whenever they heard a commotion at the corner. Once they saw a little white boy who had been thrown out of a car and was just laying there, pale in the road. Anna came out of the house and held his mother until the ambulance came.

A white woman had moved into the neighborhood when Dorothy was about eight. The neighbors called her Mrs Ski because they could not pronounce her full name. She lived with her granddaughter, who was biracial. Dorothy heard talk about the girl's mother that she did not understand, but when she asked Anna to explain it her mother told her to mind her own business. To Dorothy, the fact that Mrs Ski was white was not as remarkable as the fact that she did not have her own garden. Most Morgan Park households claimed some land, cultivating the many vacant lots in the area. The prospect of having a little land of one's own was a major attraction of the place for the mostly rural southern transplants who lived there (Chicago Commission on Race Relations 1922: 137). Mrs Rousseau regularly instructed her husband and children to share their own harvest with them. "Remember to take something over for Mrs Ski" became a common expression in the house.

Around this time a white man showed up on Mrs Robert's porch to announce that he was the new owner of the lot on which she had been planting her vegetables for more than a decade. He asked for garden rent. As Dorothy heard the story, she told him, "not in a million years." A few days later a couple of policemen showed up. Her husband told them to get off his property, and they did. "And tell him I won't pay him a dime for my garden, either!" the Roberts' neighbor, Mr. Williams, supposedly yelled to them as they drove off.[11]

Mr Estrich's store, which was in the front room of his house, was where Dorothy bought candy and crackers. The G & L was the larger grocery store where her mother bought just about everything else. Once she came home with a package of cheap bacon that outraged John. He liked to think of himself as a quiet man, but not one to be fooled with. He walked back to G & L and asked for a refund on the lard. He reminded them of that story often, and Dorothy took pride in knowing that her father would not be taken advantage of.

If we pull out further, we can capture an even wider view of Dorothy's mental geography. Across 115th Street for a long way there was nothing but the country club, race track, and golf course. Rich white people territory. Dorothy used to sneak into the track to watch the horses. "Poor people" lived around 117th Street in shacks of wood and tin that they built themselves. She knew a girl from that neighborhood, Leah, who got pregnant before she finished high school and had to drop out. Even further south, in Blue Island, there were "Mexicans." She did not know any of them. Rich white folks lived on both sides of Morgan Park. She passed their houses on the way to the library or on errands to the kosher shop in Roseland from which her parents bought live chickens, disdaining the frozen ones G & L sold. Far to the north were the slums where more poor black people lived, in brick buildings that were close together and had no yards. The bus downtown took her past some of those neighborhoods on its way to the city. They went to the Owl Theater to watch double-feature westerns, Grant Park with Mrs Rousseau to hear free public concerts, and the zoo for fun. Most of the other patrons were white, but "you stayed by yourself and they stayed by themselves" and there was "no problem."[12] At Christmas they went downtown to look at the decorations. Sometimes they shopped at Carson's, which was next to Marshall Field's, where white people bought their things. Mary Joe, who lived on 112th Street, actually worked there. Of course, she was passing. Field's did not hire black clerks.

CONCLUSION

> Goddamit, look! We live here and they live there. We black and they white. They got things and we ain't. They do things and we can't. It's like living in jail. Half the time I feel like I'm on the outside of the world peering in through a knot-hole in the fence . .

> Wright 1940: 17, *Native Sun*

Narrow mental maps, those that fail to acknowledge critical aspects of a person's environment or present a very blinkered view of reality, seem to play a role in the development of prejudicial attitudes and behaviors.[13]

A person's understanding of her social world is a cognitive construct, not a fresh, "objective" viewing of her surroundings at any given moment. The more complexity and sophistication she is able to incorporate into the maps she carries in her mind, the better equipped she will be to face others without the need to assign them to predetermined categories, and the more flexible in determining her own role in particular situations. Overly simplified, unimaginative, inelastic maps, on the other hand, are more likely to result in—indeed, to require—the reflexive pigeonholing of people and rigid interpretations of events that we associate with racist, sexist, and other destructive thinking patterns.

But what happens when the narrow maps happen to be held by members of disadvantaged groups? Might there be circumstances under which such constructs serve not antisocial but progressive purposes? Instead of instruments of bigotry, could they function as defensive or even empowering instruments of survival?

We probably expect, and research confirms, that poor children's maps will be especially circumscribed and limited.[14] Gould and White (1974: 154–5) conclude their book *Mental Maps* by worrying about the broader implications of the small worlds that the poor seem to inhabit, especially their children. What are the social costs of Latinos in East Los Angeles, for instance, of growing up in such narrowly conceived places, or blacks in Boston projects unaware of their broader surroundings? I share their concern, and at the same time this admittedly singular example gives me some hope. Dorothy certainly misunderstood the location of Morgan Park's boundaries and her ignorance of this meant that she had no framework in which to make sense of the protests that occurred at the local high school over integration or racially motivated boundary disputes about her own former elementary school, Shoop (Homel 1984: 42–4, 152–7). Indeed, she appears to have no memory of these events at all. I suspect she could not have helped but been aware of them at the time, as they occurred just blocks from her house and involved people she would have known intimately, including her older brothers. However, as she held no knowledge that helped her to make sense of these activities, she must have quickly lost interest in them.

The fact that Morgan Park High School was in the white town she called Beverly Hills did not seem strange to her, though this should have suggested that Morgan Park extended beyond the narrow borders she ascribed to it. Nor did she question having to go all the way downtown to watch movies. There were theaters closer; she must have seen them on her walks. However, they did not welcome black patrons, and she seems to have accepted that to see a movie one went to Chicago.

Something like a defiant sense of self-importance seems to have prevented Dorothy from knowing what her contemporary, Bigger Thomas, discerned clearly. I wonder about the role of my grandparents here. Did they consciously cultivate this distinctive view of Morgan Park in their children, trying to provide them with understandings and attitudes that they believed would serve them well in a racist world? Did my uncles, older and arguably more sophisticated in ways of the world, share Dorothy's geographical understanding? Perhaps her older brothers, now passed on, protective of their sisters, even contributed to creating a Morgan-Park-centered world.

Dorothy knew about the history of slavery. She grew up knowing Uncle Noah, who had been born a slave and who told her with simple dignity that there was nothing good he could say about it, so he would say nothing. She knew that throughout the country, still, black people were treated unfairly. Her father's virtual worship of A. Philip Randolph and his membership in the Pullman porters' union taught her that there were still struggles to fight. But all this was vague, and she had no sense that it had anything to do with her. "I had a pretty high opinion of myself," she says. And her description of her home is consistent with this.

> To me, it was an estate starting from our garden across the street to our garage on the alley . . . The unpaved 114th street beside our house we considered our own personal playground. Other children didn't play there without an invitation from us. It was part of our estate! The garden across the street extended our world half way up the next block. I really believe we felt our world was better and bigger than everyone else's.[15]

She did not admit any evidence from her surroundings that contradicted this.

If it is problematic that her map was a lie, it is worth remembering that no version of the world is impartial, and that some are more pernicious than others. In the 1950s Interstate 57 was extended through Morgan Park, just east of Vincennes Ave. Since then, the white civic elite of Morgan Park has redefined the suburb to exclude what falls on the other side of the freeway, the swathe it cuts allowing a convenient opportunity for dropping the one-third of the community that happens to be black off the map (Figure 4). The Chamber of Commerce, Historical Society, and other local groups have recast Morgan Park as the neighborhood of gracious, "historic" homes on the ridge, pushing the African-American rest into "Chicago."

This redrawing of boundaries, of course, has the effect of rewriting history. If Morgan Park is cast as a town that has always been well-off and white, there can have been no need in the past to impose racial segregation there, nor any now to acknowledge the practices by which earlier residents achieved this. Race and class distinctions are naturalized, just as they were in Dorothy's map, though in an ironic inverse of her scheme. The racial borders, which still exist, are rendered innocent occurrences rather than the result of contrived policies. Indeed, as we might expect, modern accounts of Morgan Park's past do not even mention its former African-American residents, let alone the segregation that white residents imposed on them.[16] Dorothy's maps and the new official versions achieve the same purpose: they erase a past of

Figure 4
Comparison of Dorothy's
mental map with modern
elite conceptualization.
Dorothy's mental map of
Morgan Park's location
relative to neighboring
Beverly Hills and other
surrounding white areas is a
mirror image of the current
elite version. Both recognize
the racial border, but each
makes its own claim about
what side of that border
Morgan Park falls on.
Drawing: Janet Stephens.

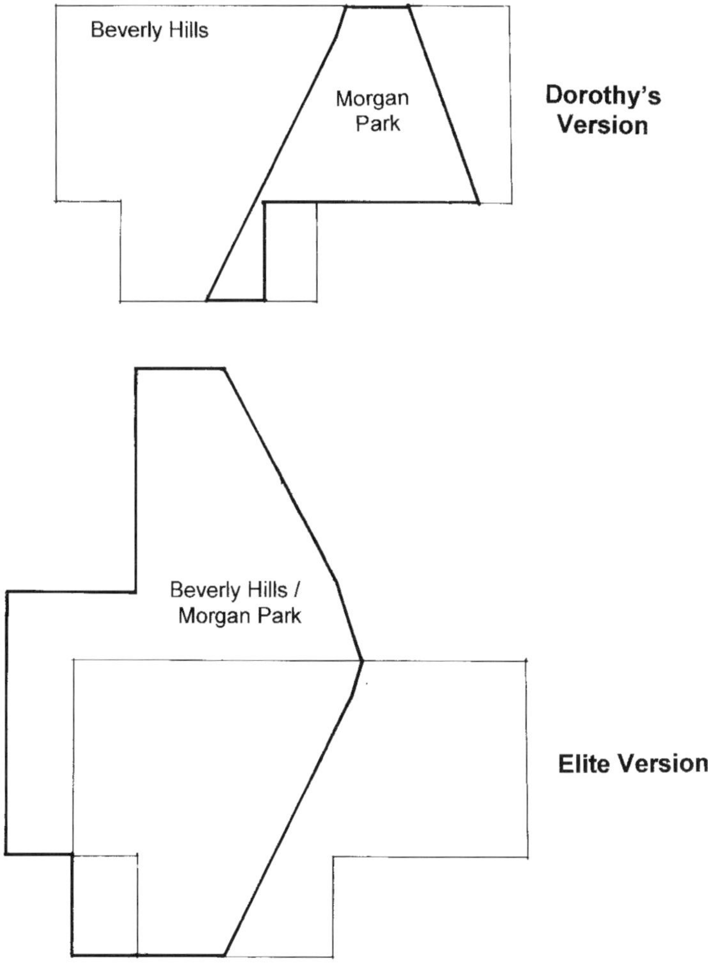

racial tension and discrimination. The silence is more becoming in the victim.

ACKNOWLEDGMENTS

When I wrote this article I was a postdoctoral fellow in the African and Afro-American Studies Program at Washington University in St Louis. I am grateful for all its support, especially for the services of my illustrator, Janet Stephens. Thank you to Janet, and thank you most of all to my mother, Dorothy Rousseau Ginsburg.

NOTES

1. I use the terms "landscapes" and "mental maps" interchangeably here. On environmental knowing generally, see Downs and Stea (1973), Gould and White (1974), Lynch (1960), Moore and Golledge (1976), and Pocock and Hudson (1978).

2. See, for example, Clark (1986), Foy and Schlereth (1992), and Gowans (1986). But see also Wright (1981), whose history of American housing includes a chapter on black urban neighborhoods. There are also several good studies, many contemporary, of working-class, ethnic, white domestic life. Though their focus is not upon architecture as such, many address housing conditions and domestic technologies. See, for example, Bodnar (1982), Byington (1910), Eastman (1927), and Lynd and Merrell Lynd (1929). Borchert (1980), McDaniel (1982), which focuses on tenant families, and Wade (1964) are among the few studies that address black American domestic life and material conditions, though they do not address northern, twentieth-century urban conditions.

3. I conducted fourteen interviews with my mother, DRG, on the following dates: March 12 1993, March 16 1993, March 17 1993, March 19 1993, March 22 1993, March 23 1993, March 24 1993, March 25 1993, March 13 1996, September 22 2002, January 5 2003, January 6 2003, April 28 2003, May 3 2003. All but the six earliest were tape-recorded. Citing has been challenging, since so many of the same points were repeated during different interviews as well as during phone calls and visits with my mother. For the sake of simplification, then, and ease of reading I have chosen only to cite direct quotations.

4. In fact, until I started to research Morgan Park and report my findings to her, my mother still believed that it had been a predominantly black town. Her exact words, when I first told her I had discovered that whites in fact formed the majority, were, "There were whites there? Where were they?" (telephone conversation with author, June 10 2003).

5. On the incorporation of Chicago's suburbs generally, see Keating (1988).

6. On the tendency of migrants to move first to the Black Belt and then, if possible, to other neighborhoods, see Spear (1967: 132) and Grossman (1989: 143). On the Chicago migration generally, see Spear (1967), Grossman (1989), Chicago Commission on Race Relations (1922, Chapter 3: "The Migration of Negroes from the South") and Frazier (1932, Chapter 5: "When the Negro Family Moves to the City" and Chapter 6: "The Negro Community in Chicago"), Black (2003), and Philpott (1991).

7. On white response to black migration in Chicago see Spear (1967, especially Chapter 11: "Migration and the White Response") and Chicago Commission on Race Relations (1922).

8. Apartments rented for a little more than US$25 in the black area of Morgan Park compared to US$22.74 in the densest area of the Black Belt in 1940 (Chicago Plan Commission 1942: 22, 77). The greatest impediment to moving to Morgan Park, though, was not price but availability.

9. For 1910 and 1920 figures, see Chicago Commission on Race Relations (1922: 107); for 1940 figure, population calculated from Chicago Plan Commission (1942: 4, 77).
10. Tape recording, interview, DRG, May 3 2003.
11. Tape recording, interview, DRG, May 3 2003. Since my mother does not seem to have been present at any of the scenes, I assume this story has grown in the telling of it. It appears to have become a neighborhood legend, and one that bolstered the sense of ownership and control Morgan Park residents and their children had over their homes.
12. Tape recording, interview, DRG, March 24 1993.
13. Edward Tolman, the Berkeley psychologist who cognitive or mental maps (I use the terms interchangeably here) in rats articulated his concern about the possible repercussions of holding narrow maps in a now-classic paper (Tolman 1948). Others have subsequently explored the links between cognition and the development of racist attitudes, in particular. See, for example, Aboud (1988).
14. See, for example, Gould and White (1974: 14–19) for examples of studies that confirm this.
15. DRG letter, February 18 1992.
16. See, for example, the history of the area presented at the Ridge Historical Society (RHS) website, at www.ridgehistoricalsociety.org and the Beverly Area Planning Association, www.bapa.org. Harold Wolfe of the RHS confirms that what used to be called East Morgan Park is no longer considered part of the suburb, telephone interview, June 12 2003.

REFERENCES

Aboud, Frances. 1988. *Children and Prejudice.* London: Basil Blackwell.

Black, Timvel D. 2003. *Bridges of Memory: Chicago's First Wave of Black Migration*. Evanston, IL: Northwestern University Press.

Bodnar, John. 1982. *Workers' World: Kinship, Community, and Protest in an Industrial Society, 1900–1940.* Baltimore, MD: Johns Hopkins University Press.

Borchert, James. 1980. *Alley Life in Washington: Family, Community, Religion, and Folklife in the City, 1850–1970.* Urbana, IL: University of Illinois Press.

Byington, Margaret Frances. 1910. *Homestead: The Households of a Mill Town.* New York: Charities Publication Committee.

Chicago Commission on Race Relations, The. 1922. *The Negro in Chicago: A Study of Race Relations and a Race Riot.* Chicago, IL: University of Chicago Press.

Chicago Plan Commission, The. 1942. *Forty-Four Cities in the City of Chicago.* Chicago, IL: The Chicago Plan Commission.

Clark, Clifford Edward. 1986. *The American Family Home, 1800–1960.* Chapel Hill, NC: University of North Carolina Press.

Downs, Roger and David Stea (eds). 1973. *Cognitive Mapping and Spatial Behavior.* Chicago, IL: Aldine Publishing Company.

Eastman, Inc. 1927. *Zanesville and 36 Other American Communities: A Study of Markets and of the Telephone as a Market Index.* New York: Literary Digest.

Frazier, E. Franklin. 1932. *The Negro Family in Chicago.* Chicago, IL: University of Chicago Press.

Foy, Jessica H. and Thomas J. Schlereth (eds). 1992. *American Home Life, 1880–1930: A Social History of Spaces and Services.* Knoxville, TN: University of Tennessee Press.

Gould, Peter and Rodney White. 1974. *Mental Maps.* New York: Penguin Books.

Gowans, Alan. 1986. *The Comfortable House: North American Suburban Architecture, 1890–1930.* Cambridge, MA: MIT Press.

Grossman, James Rousseau. 1989. *Land of Hope: Chicago, Black Southerners, and the Great Migration.* Chicago, IL: University of Chicago Press.

Hansberry, Lorraine. 1958. *A Raisin in the Sun: A Drama in Three Acts.* New York: Random House.

Homel, Michael W. 1984. *Down From Equality: Black Chicagoans and the Public Schools, 1920–41*, pp. 152–7. Urbana, IL: University of Illinois Press.

Keating, Ann Durkin. 1988. *Building Chicago: Suburban Developers and the Creation of a Divided Metropolis.* Columbus, OH: Ohio State University Press.

Lynch, Kevin. 1960. *The Image of the City.* Cambridge, MA: MIT Press.

Lynd, Robert S. and Helen Merrell Lynd. 1929. *Middletown: A Study in Contemporary American Culture.* New York: Harcourt, Brace and Co.

McDaniel, George W. 1982. *Hearth and Home: Preserving a People's Culture.* Philadelphia, PA: Temple University Press.

Moore, Gary T. and Reginald Golledge. 1976. *Environmental Knowing: Theories, Research, and Methods.* Stroudsbourg, PA: Dowden, Hutchinson, & Ross.

Philpott, Thomas Lee. 1991. *The Slum and the Ghetto: Immigrants, Blacks and Reformers in Chicago, 1880–1930.* Belmont, CA: Wadswoth Publishing Co.

Pocock, Douglas and Ray Hudson. 1978. *Images of the Urban Environment.* New York: Columbia University Press.

Spear, Allan H. 1967. *Black Chicago: The Making of a Negro Ghetto, 1890–1920.* Chicago, IL: University of Chicago Press.

Tolman, Edward. 1948. "Cognitive Maps in Rats and Men." *Psychological Review* July 1948.

Wade, Richard. 1964. *Slavery in the Cities: The South, 1820–1860.* Oxford: Oxford University Press.

Wright, Richard. 1940. *Native Son.* New York: Harper & Brothers Publishers.

Wright, Gwendolyn. 1981. *Building the Dream: A Social History of Housing in America.* New York: Pantheon Books.

HOME CULTURES VOLUME 1, ISSUE 2. PP 147–168

CHIARA BRIGANTI AND KATHY MEZEI

HOUSE HAUNTING: THE DOMESTIC NOVEL OF THE INTER-WAR YEARS[1]

CHIARA BRIGANTI IS PROFESSOR OF ENGLISH AND WOMEN'S AND GENDER STUDIES AT CARLETON COLLEGE, MINNESOTA. SHE DIVIDES HER TIME BETWEEN THE UNITED STATES AND ENGLAND. HER SPECIAL FIELDS OF INTEREST ARE THE VICTORIAN NOVEL AND MODERNISM AND MODERNITY. SHE AND KATHY MEZEI HAVE EDITED A SPECIAL FORUM OF SIGNS (SPRING 2002) ON DOMESTIC SPACE AND ARE COLLABORATING ON A PROJECT CONCERNING THE DOMESTIC NOVEL AND DOMESTIC SPACE.

KATHY MEZEI IS PROFESSOR OF HUMANITIES AND ENGLISH AT SIMON FRASER UNIVERSITY IN VANCOUVER, B.C., AND SPECIALIZES IN DOMESTIC SPACE, TRANSLATION STUDIES, CANADIAN LITERATURES, AND MODERN BRITISH WOMEN WRITERS. SHE AND CHIARA BRIGANTI ARE COLLABORATING ON A PROJECT CONCERNING THE DOMESTIC NOVEL AND DOMESTIC SPACE. SHE HAS RECENTLY GUEST-EDITED A SPECIAL ISSUE OF BC STUDIES (WINTER 2003–4) ON "DOMESTIC SPACES" AND INVITES YOU TO PARTICIPATE IN THE DOMETIC SPACE WEBSITE: WWW.SFU.CA/DOMESTIC-SPACE.

In this article we attempt to historicize and address the literary manifestations of the meaning and idea of home culture in the English domestic novel of the inter-war years. During this period, the cult of domesticity was avidly promoted by the government and popular magazines. We discuss how both houses and novels furnish a dwelling place that invites the exploration of private and social relations. In their turn to domestic space and the domestic interior, domestic novelists of the inter-war years inaugurated a turn to interiority, feminine subjectivity and the everyday.

Thought cannot want its house. But the house haunts it.

Lyotard 1999: 277

"Must the novel be a house?"

Bhabha 1997: 446

Indeed, as strongly as thought might resist its house, the house does haunt it, as the very etymology of the verb suggests. For if in English one of the meanings of "haunt" is a "place or abode that one frequents" (its origins lie in the Old English "hamettan," to provide with a home or house), in French, "hantise" carries the connotation of an obsession, a nagging memory (Derrida 1994: 177, note 2). Keeping in mind this mixing of obsession, home, and memory, one could argue that houses are stories and narratives of hauntings by memories, ghosts, traces of selves and others, while stories are haunted by fictional and lived and imagined houses, which frequently mimic the psyche and bodies of their inhabitants as well as the social practices and political ideologies, the *habitus* (see Bourdieu 1990: 53) of the nation. Gaston Bachelard's seminal study *The Poetics of Space* teases out such reciprocity by acknowledging the haunting of house by book and book by house when he reflects how "we write a room," "read a room," or "read a house" (Bachelard 1994: 14). Similarly, if less explicitly, Jacques Derrida's concept of the logic of hauntology ("hantise"), which points to the relationship between the first time and the last time of an event, to repetition and return, and to the spectral sense of the presence of "someone as someone other," resonates with the repetitions, returns, and hauntology of the act of writing and reading the novel and of being in the house (Derrida 1994: 9, 10).

This article attempts to historicize and address the literary manifestations of the meaning and idea of home culture in the English domestic novel of the inter-war years, a period whose "single most arresting feature . . . was the strength of the notion that women's place is in the home" (Beddoe 1989: 3).[2] The idea of home became a hotly contested topic as a "return to the home" was promoted by government both through propaganda and policies of subsidized housing, suburban villas and mass housing, "homes fit for heroes;" by events such as the Ideal Home Exhibitions and programs like the BBC's *Woman's Hour*; as well as by women's magazines (*Good Housekeeping*, *Woman and Home*, *My Home*, *Modern Home*), which featured articles and advertisements on homemaking, interior decoration, and labor-saving devices.[3] During this same period, the domestic novel written by middle-class women for middle-class women about middle-class women [and often middle-aged women] (Beauman 1983: 3) became a popular genre, its success facilitated by the growth of lending libraries, cheaper publications in the form of reprints, paperbacks, and book societies, and the unprecedented growth of women's magazines.

THE HOUSE OF FICTION

> A strong concern with architecture signifies in fiction as it does outside a concern with protection, a desire for established existence and a home for consciousness (Harbison 2000: 73).

How do we understand the history and representations of the symbiosis of house and novel as signaled here by Harbison? In other words, how do we account for the persistent haunting of houses by novels, and novels by houses? For the novel itself could be described as a domestic space, one of a variety of species in which built forms (houses, laboratories, offices, boarding schools, retirement homes—and their gardens, borders, and interiors and furnishings) interact with domestic lives. Within the novel, domestic spaces frequently serve as the medium of negotiation and communication between author, characters, and reader, and between self and other, and with the self.[4]

Both home and novel are constructions which represent, imitate, and enable people to live, interact, engage publicly or retreat into privacy since with the rise of the leisured, moneyed middle class the house became a "setting for an emerging interior life" (Rybczynski 1986: 35–6). Thus, for inter-war writers like Virginia Woolf and Katherine Mansfield, who foreground home culture in their experimental fictions, novels *and* houses furnish a dwelling place that invites the exploration and expression of private and intimate relations and thoughts. Their use of private domestic space as frame and metonym of inner, psychological space reflects the recent (nineteenth-century) validation of privacy and intimacy. For example, in Woolf's *To the Lighthouse* (1927), the reader enters into the Ramsay children's consciousness by entering their nursery. Similarly, at the end of Part One, the end of a long day in the Ramsay summer house, the reader, along with Mrs Ramsay, moves into the drawing room with Mrs Ramsay as she joins her husband and into the intimacy of their marriage. In modern and contemporary novels, representations of the domestic interior mirror the inner thoughts of women, children, servants, those "spectral" dwellers within the house who may appear to be at home in this space, although even this domestic space has been designed and controlled by the patriarchy.

Readers repeatedly encounter the architectural in fiction, the importance of the home, and houses as personae. For not only do writers place a "building at the center of a book in order to provide the scaffolding of automatic organization" (Harbison 2000: 74), but they also frequently refer to their work as a built form and to their writing in terms of building. Describing her radical "method" in *Mrs Dalloway*, Woolf resorts to architectural metaphors: ". . . her [Woolf's] dissatisfaction was primarily with nature for giving an idea, without providing a house for it to live in . . . [For the novelists of the preceding generation] the novel was the obvious lodging, but the novel it seemed was built on the wrong plan" (Woolf 1928: 36).

Throughout literary history, critics too have described literature and the process of writing in architectural terms: thus Walter Pater talks of "literary architecture," Henry James of the "house of fiction," while Pierre Bourdieu refers to the house as a book in which is inscribed a vision and structure of society and the world (Carsten and Hugh-Jones 1995: 2). Frederic Jameson queries whether built space (comprising rooms, corridors, doorways) is a kind of language, and investigates the re-narrativization of domestic space and the family in modernity in "Is Space Political?" (1999: 261). Similarly, Sharon Marcus (1999) notes how "narration itself (and not simply the events narrated) inscribes spatial relations" (p. 10), and in his study of dislocation, Homi Bhabha (1997) reminds us that, "the image of the house has always been used to talk about the expansive, mimetic nature of the novel" (p. 446) (see also Mezei and Briganti 2002a: 837–46). In her analogical model, Philippa Tristram describes the novel as invincibly domestic because it functions like the house as a little world we think we can control (1989: 2). Tristram calls attention to the correspondences between domestic architecture, which can reveal hidden aspects of the novelist's art, and novels; these correspondences are manifest in terms like structure, aspect, outlook, character, content, liminal, threshold, entry point, perspective, kitchen sink drama, drawing-room comedy, aga saga, country house mysteries, cosies (detective novels), the locked room mystery, and the domestic novel.[5]

Although, as Ellen Eve Frank's (1979) *Literary Architecture* demonstrates, this habit of comparison between architecture and literature extends from Plato to Samuel Beckett (p. 9), it was during the great age of the English house in the eighteenth and early nineteenth century when, not surprisingly, house portraiture was a "favored art form among the wealthy" (Garber 2000: 39) that a recurring phenomenon—the symbolic relationship between house and novel—consolidated itself. In the nineteenth century iconic houses such as Mansfield Park stand for Englishness and nation. However, in the early twentieth century, encroaching industrialization and modernization, along with nostalgia for fading nationhood, class privilege, and imperial power, haunt the disturbed spaces of Brideshead (Evelyn Waugh, *Brideshead Revisited*, 1945), Howards End (E. M. Forster, *Howards End*, 1970 [1910]), Manderley (Daphne du Maurier, *Rebecca*, 1938), and Danielstown (Elizabeth Bowen, *The Last September*, 1979 [1929]). At the same time, boarding houses and bedsits, hybrid of public and private spaces, "a home from home" (Hall 1959: 107), which in the inter-war novels of Jean Rhys, Laura Talbot, E. H. Young and many others, so often shelter single women of faded gentility, are a reminder not only of the decline of great houses and the upper classes, but also of the decimation of the male population by the war that affected the destiny of so many women. Thus, Aunt Ellen, elderly, single, alone reflects about Miss Russell's boarding house in Lettice Cooper's (1987 [1936]) *The New House*: "Because this was not a real house, but a place of hire and bargain, people were supplied with the minimum of everything they would put up with" (p. 282).[6]

However, it was not only the decline of the upper classes and the sad fate of the "surplus" woman that the architecture of the novel registered; it also ambivalently acknowledged the rise of a more urban, middle-class, mobile society. Some characters in inter-war domestic novels, like Celia in E. H. Young's 1937 eponymous novel, while lamenting the loss of "beauty in the world," accept with equanimity the disappearance of "servants living in the underground vaults, [their] legs aching with going up and down these stairs, from basement to attics and attics to basement" (Young 1990 [1937]: 33). More frequently, though, characters echo the regret of the Schlegel sisters in *Howards End* at the turning of great country homes and estates into public museums or housing "estates" and the growth of "nasty little red houses, full of common people and screaming children, all over that lovely garden" (Cooper 1987 [1936]: 41). Lettice Cooper and Rose Macaulay are gently satirical toward the accepted premise of life that "suburbans are dull" (Macaulay 1967 [1926]: 111) and the simple solution to the housing problem that "working people should have decent houses but not in any place that would spoil the view for our sort of people" (Cooper 1987 [1936]: 41). Elizabeth Bowen, on the other hand, is uncompromisingly stringent in her censure of the new middle class as seen through their dwellings: in *The Heat of the Day* (1949) Stella pointedly identifies the pretentious neo-Gothic architecture of suburban Holme Dene with the moral emptiness of its inhabitants and her lover's propensity for betrayal.

THE INTER-WAR CULT OF THE HOUSE

During the period between the two World Wars, the modernist movement apparently rejected the drearily domestic summarized in Le Corbusier's critique of the "cult of the house." Indeed, as Rita Felski has argued, "[t]he vocabulary of modernity is a vocabulary of anti-home" (Felski 1999–2000: 23). In their turn to domestic spaces many female domestic novelists were negotiating, in their technique and their subject matter, the modernist antipathy to the home as exemplified by Le Corbusier, the brilliant celebration of domestic decoration and house objects by the Bloomsbury artists of the Omega Workshop, and government-sponsored, market-driven, consumer-fueled propaganda for a postwar "cult of domesticity."

The turn to the home and the domestic interior between the wars and a corresponding turn in the novel form is hardly surprising. Similarly to the eighteenth century, which saw the rise of the novel, the inter-war period also experienced a domestication, feminization, and privatization of society.[7] New feminism, which gained ground in the 1920s, attempted to "develop a new, more domestically oriented feminist ideology" and to improve the situation of women in the home to the dismay of Old Feminists like Winifred Holtby, who felt that this was a revival of the traditional image of women as domestic, mother, housewife, and wife (Trodd 1998: 5). Social historian John Burnett notes that new recruits to the middle class, which increased from 20.3% of the total population in 1911 to 30.4% in 1951, "shared with the older members of the class the belief that family and home were the central life interests, and that the house, which enshrined these institutions, had an importance far beyond other material objects" (Burnett 1986: 251). The demand for middle-class housing and council estates, the growth of suburbs and garden cities outside London—an attempt to protect the countryside from suburban sprawl (Wilson 1991: 100)—with its concomitant proliferation of detached, single-family houses, engendered a taste for home life and an economy of homemaking. Within the domestic interiors of these houses and novels, women and children were discovering and forging separate and legitimatized identities. The paperback revolution highlighted by Allen Lane's 1935 revolutionary Penguins boosted the publication and distribution of women's novels. For example, one-third of the "Fiction —orange covers" series in "Penguin Book's Complete List of Publications to the End of 1938" were popular women novelists including: Phyllis Bottome, Susan Ertz, Stella Gibbons, Ethel Mannin, E. Arnot Robertson, Vita Sackville-West, Beatrice Kean Seymour, Angela Thirkell, Sylvia Townsend Warner, and E.H. Young.[8] Interestingly the "History of Modern Design in the Home" exhibit at the Design Museum[9] linked the modern home to the Penguin paperback, claiming that both the Penguins and the Lawn Road Flats, London service flats built in 1932 in the continental international style, were infused with the same democratic spirit of improving the quality of people's lives.[10]

Although the English pastoral continued to play an important part in fiction and poetry (Mary Webb, Sheila Kaye-Smith, E. Arnot Robertson, Dodie Smith), modernity, the metropolis, and the home, whether rural or urban, replaced the pastoral idyll as a site for the emerging feminine self. As many women architects were guided towards the design of houses and contributed to develop "a tradition of modernist 'social' architecture, with holiday camps and nurseries" (Wilson 1991: 93), so women novelists in the inter-war years became increasingly preoccupied with what Nicola Humble has called "imagining the home" (pp. 109–48). The experience of the First World War, the resultant trauma of instability and the desire for recuperation, which coexisted with a resistance to a "return to normality," both enhanced the idea and meaning of home for returning soldiers and the home front and accentuated that crisis of gender relations which had been brewing for decades. Laurence Storm, Storm Jameson's protagonist in *Three Kingdoms* (1926), responds to her husband's claim that "[a]s the world gets more settled, less women will need to work, and one by one they'll fall back thankfully on some man. It's their instinct" (p. 181), by retorting: "You're wrong . . . More and more girl children are being born like me, with an instinct for freedom and to get out . . . You talk about our apathy and forget the tradition behind us. Back of men are memories of the outside of the cave. Back of women are only memories of the inside. We're out. We're out now. You'll never push us back" (p. 181).

Not for lack of attempts, though. A "return to the home" was energetically promoted through the commercial sphere—advertisements

Figure 1
"Come and See Lawn Road Flats." Design for advertisement c. 1934. Photograph courtesy of the Pritchard Archive, University of East Anglia.

and the growing number of women's magazines. These magazines—*Good Housekeeping*, 1922; *Modern Woman*, 1925; *Everywoman's*, 1934; *Woman and Home*, 1926; *My Home*, 1928; *Modern Home*, 1928; *Woman's Journal*, 1927—which competed for middle- and lower-middle-class women consumers were "dedicated . . . to upholding the traditional sphere of feminine interests and . . . recommending a purely domestic role for women" (White 1970: 100).[11] Featuring articles which focused on homemaking rather than on high society, and advertisements on interior decoration and labor-saving devices, they were informed by the same ideology that supported the government-sponsored postwar program of social reconstruction. As a random sample, the April 1932 (31:2) issue of *Good Housekeeping*, ran articles on "Suburban Flats

Planned to Save Labour," and "The Art of Waiting at Table," while in response to this trend, *The Lady* and *The Queen* shifted their emphasis from society women to the middle class. Events like the Ideal Home Exhibitions and programs like the BBC's *Woman's Hour* also glorified the idea of home and women's domestic sphere (Chapman and Hockey 1999: 1–13; Humble 2001: 108–18; Trodd 1998: 5). With the marriage bar, women were forced to turn and return to the home after marriage; symptomatically, *The Lady* cut its employment features and substituted homemaking articles (White 1970: 100). In 1932, *Good Housekeeping* published a story by Prudence O'Shea, "The Happiest Way of Things," the story of a wife who had to choose whether to run a job or a home, and chose to be a wife; however, in April 1930, it had also published provocative articles by Vera Brittain on the subject "Why I Think Mothers Can Have Careers" and by Storm Jameson in June 1927 on "Marriage," which she calls the "The Most Difficult Profession in the World." Brittain (1930: 146) firmly supports careers for women, noting that "[m]any people still object that such experiments will mean the neglect of children and the ruin of the home. I can only reply, after having experimented in this way myself, that I don't believe it. I have known several homes come to grief, but they were all spoilt by wives who had too little, not too much, to do." Pointing out that wifehood and motherhood are not jobs, she then reminds the reader that "like husbandhood and fatherhood," wifehood and motherhood "are intimate and sacred relationships, which exist quite independently of the economic occupation, whatever this may be, of the person who adopts them" (p. 147).

Resisting the facile glamorization of the housewife, domestic novelists engaged in a thoughtful, often lyrical, witty reclamation of domesticity and the home. They simultaneously privileged and critiqued the home and homemaking, at times resenting the demands of the family on the "domesticated female," like Norah in Lehmann's *A Note in Music* (1982 [1930]), "Only, tonight she hated the active life, wanted to have a rest from this perpetual crumbling of the edges, this shredding out of one's personality upon minute obligations and responsibilities" (p. 52), but often also imbuing the home with lyrical and evocative qualities. The resulting textualization of the house and home offered women writers a pattern within which to write or against which to write.[12]

HOUSE, NOVEL, BODY

By embodying the house, inter-war domestic novelists appropriated a tradition that represents architecture in terms of an organic structure, its dimensions and scale modeled on the human body. This tradition originates with Vitruvius's prescription that the temple "must have an exact proportion worked out after the fashion of the members of a finely shaped human body" (Garber 2000: 73–4). In her recent contribution to this tradition, Marjorie Garber for instance discusses how the representation of the house as a human body in arts and theology has emphasized one of three "organic" elements—proportion, function, or sex and gender roles (p. 73).[13] House, body, and mind are in continuous interaction, the physical structure, furniture, social rituals, and mental images of the house at once enabling, molding, informing, and constraining the activities and ideas which unfold within its bounds (Carsten and Hugh-Jones 1995: 2). Thus, in Rebecca West's *Harriet Hume* (1980 [1929]), "the dumpy windows of the 'best bedroom' floor," the "dining-room windows, broad and slightly protuberant, like the paunch of a moderate over-eater" of the houses in Kensington are a suitable introduction to a "fat papa," a "fat mamma" (pp. 7, 8), and fat progeny and do much to conjure up a future of dismal self-complacency for Arnold and Harriet.

In extending the idea of house and body to include the gendering and sexualizing of the house, Garber suggests that the "house has been simply and directly mapped onto the female body" (2000: 49), partly an extension of the cult of domesticity, partly a literal reading of women's sexuality as something enclosed and interior. Thus, not only is the well-established identification of mother and home as expressed in Richard Hoggart's recollections of growing up in a working-class family in the North of England (quoted in Morley 2000: 63), where "Ma" is "the pivot of the home," but the house itself may be embodied as mother, as the figures of Mrs Ramsay in *To the Lighthouse* (1927) and Mrs Wilcox in *Howards End* (1910) poignantly suggest. When these maternal figures die, the "house itself seems to die as well" (Garber 2000: 59). Repeatedly in inter-war domestic novels, the house and the mother come to symbolize the oppression and repression of young women's independent selves as they are obligated to and, in some cases, welcome the charge of houses and widowed mothers. The heroines of Lettice Cooper's *The New House* (1987 [1936]), May Sinclair's *Mary Olivier: A Life* (1919), Radclyffe Hall's *The Unlit Lamp* (1981 [1924]), E. M. Delafield's *Thank Heaven Fasting* (1989 [1932]) are torn between their desire for freedom and their duty to an often manipulative mother and high-maintenance house, mediated by fear of independence and the public world. By the time Roland Pertwee's *School for Spinsters* was produced in London in 1947, the plight of the daughter manipulated into a life of service by parents "like . . . lampreys which suck the life-blood out of people" (p. 65), had become a stock character. While in *The New House*, Aunt Ellen's wasted life had provided an unwitting warning to Rhoda, in this play the spinster aunt Prudence uses her experience to caution Rose against a life of potting "along behind the greedy old people who turned us into slaves" (Pertwee 1948: 40).

HOUSE, OBJECTS, AGENCY

In the domestic novel, furniture and ornaments act as ritualized forms of communication, and assume fetishistic roles. In E. M. Delafield's *Thank Heaven Fasting* (1989 [1932]), the décor of Monica's bedroom is "a silent testimony that violent and radical change held no place in her life;" for though Monica, as a faded woman of thirty, has long ceased to be the blooming *débutante* who had filled her parents with pride, she is still surrounded by "[p]ink silk, brass, and white-painted furniture" (p. 174). In Ada Leverson's (1982 [1908–16]) *The Little Ottleys* not only is the phrase "little Ottleys," which describes Edith and Bruce, emphasized by repeated references to their "very small . . . flat in Knightsbridge" (p. 33), but the affinity between certain characters is suggested by their preference in room arrangements and the taste in decoration they share. Edith's unostentatious unconventionality, reflected in her dislike for traditional dark dining-rooms and chilly, ceremonious drawing-rooms, is paralleled by Lord Selsey's flouting "of the ordinary subdivisions of a house:" "he did not see why one should breakfast in a breakfast-room, dine in a dining-room, draw in a drawing-room, and so on" (p. 73). Even more suggestively, the "feminine curves of the furniture" (p. 394) Edith has chosen are suitably contrasted with the masculine quality of her lover's room: "[I]t was essentially a man's room. Comfortable, but not exactly luxurious; very little was sacrificed to decoration" (p. 450).

Rooms not only reflect the personalities of their inhabitants, they also serve as jumping-off points for stories about the self as in the celebrated opening of Dodie Smith's, *I Capture the Castle*: "I write this sitting in the kitchen sink" (1976, [1948]: 3) as well as foreshadowing events. In E. Arnot Robertson's *Cullum* (1989 [1928]), the background to the heroine's second encounter with the man who will betray her is "a dull room, sparsely furnished . . . which had just missed the good asceticism in style that had been attempted, and was only hard and coldly refined, like a plain, unintentional virgin" (p. 16).

Specific domestic spaces emphatically position characters and readers. And, since it makes a difference to the "story" whether the reader enters by the front door or the side door and who stands where on the staircase, liminal spaces such as windows, stairs, and doors not only determine focalization, but also perform strategic narrative functions of drawing readers into the story or into the character's thoughts. Furthermore such spaces also stand emblematic of social intercourse and the transition between public and private space. So, for instance, in Young's (1947) *Chatterton Square*, Mr Blackett's dread of the doorstep as a dangerous point of neighborly invasion reflects this character's parochialism; whereas in *Celia*, the title character's social astuteness is suggested by the narrator's comment that Celia's ear is "tuned to every step on the stairs, to each different manner of turning the key in the lock and opening and shutting the door" (Young 1990 [1927]: 81). With a different symbolic valence to this grammar of the house, elderly Mrs Swithin in Virginia Woolf's 1941 *Between the Acts* alludes to the staircase of life, "this daily round; this going up and down stairs" (Woolf 1970 [1941]: 152), a sentiment echoed by Young in the narrator's iteration of Celia continuously climbing the stairs, which signals the onerous repetitiveness of her life.

Edouard Vuillard's words, "I don't make portraits. I paint people in their homes,"[14] could have been uttered by many inter-war domestic novelists, whose subject is often a figure in the carpet, which can only be grasped by carefully disentangling the threads of familial relationships grounded in and through specific domestic spaces. Indeed, the fascination of the domestic, family networks, attentiveness to mundane tasks and simple acts, constitutes a strong link between the domestic novelist and that pictorial tradition that leads from the Netherlands to the England of Duncan Grant and Vanessa Bell and to the France of Vuillard and Pierre Bonnard. In paintings and novels, the everyday, domestic objects, and interiors perform as "effective ideological carriers" of culture and society, making ideology transparent (Langbauer 1999: 7). One has only to think of Johannes Vermeer's and Pieter de Hooch's Dutch interiors with their symbolic mirrors, doorways, women reading letters, and cast aside brooms and buckets suggestive of domesticity, illicit sex, and the desire to escape domesticity. Each of these works encapsulates "the slog of daily life, the tussle between compulsion and habit" (Shone 2000: 57). Richard Shone notes how in Vermeer's picture of a woman pouring milk, "temporal erosion and the boredom of domestic continuity give tension to [a] superficially tranquil image of daily life" (p. 56); while Susan Sidlauskas notes how, in the paintings of Bonnard and Vuillard, house objects are invested with a sort of "animacy" (1996: 71). Such "animacy" lends an edge to Rose Macaulay's satire of household routines in *Crewe Train* (1967 [1926]), where the household hints that Audrey bestows on the newly-wed Denham and Arnold ("about how to keep the kettle from furring, and the stove and the milk jar from smelling") are aimed at "keep[ing] the things in the house from behaving as is natural to their species" (p. 154). On a less benignant note, Sidlauskas's comments on how the oversized furniture in Vuillard's "Mother and Sister of the Artist" exaggerates the narrowness of the space and adds to the "all over sense of constriction" (1996: 73) could very well apply to Celia's bedroom, where she feels as equally crowded in by her husband's hovering bulk as by the massive carved furniture that he has brought from his paternal home, "the wardrobe like some large animal" (p. 101) and the barbaric bed (p. 17).

HANTISE

In the works of novelists attuned to the grammar of the home, houses, and the material objects they contain are not merely passive expressions of agency or mirrors of the people who live in them or own them, but serve as "the site of memory and of our formative experiences" (Bird 2000 [1995]: 112). Imprinted by the body, they become "vessels of memory and touchstones of experience" (Shone 2000: 55), a body space, so to speak. The "toutounier" in Colette's 1939 novella by the same name is a veritable womb-like nest of female intimacy, to which the Eudes sisters repeatedly "return" to speak a private language and repair the ravages wrought by poverty and emotional exhaustion. In the English tradition of novels by Elizabeth Bowen, Rosamond Lehmann, Elizabeth von Arnim, E. M. Delafield, Virginia Woolf, and Enid Bagnold, houses and their accoutrements become living beings with names and personalities as in the haunted space of Pinderwell House in E. H. Young's *Moor Fires* (1916), where the rooms have been named after Mr Pinderwell's unborn children. Storehouses of memory, repression, and desires, these domestic spaces speak of the hold of the past on the lives of the characters. In Young's *Jenny Wren* (1985 [1932]), not only does Jenny's dead father's bureau become a commodity of exchange in the fluctuating relationship between Jenny Rendall and Edwin Cummings, it also haunts Jenny with a paternal legacy of unattainable taste and status. Thus, as Bird (2000 [1995]) notes "[s]imple objects reveal ambiguities that shift their identity and introduce an element of uncertainty. Invested with shared meanings—the functions of the body, familial experience, the patterns of everyday life—they are sufficiently strange to avoid the closure that accompanies classification, like a memory trace that hovers at the edge of recall" (p. 112). In Mollie Panter-Downes's post-World War Two novel, *One Fine Day* (1985 [1947]), one character recalls what a dreadful job it is to abandon a house where "so many people had saved and stored everything carefully for centuries, letters, journals, estate accounts, locks of hair, shreds of silk, sentimental rubbish of all sorts" (p. 117). But it is in Bowen that we find the most fully articulated expression of "hantise." In her story, "The New House," the spinster protagonist utters a paradigmatic complaint: "Why, even the way the furniture was arranged at No. 17 held me so that I couldn't get away. The way the chairs went in the sitting-room. And mother" (Bowen 1980: 57). In Bowen's *The Last September* (1979 [1929]), as Maud Ellmann (2001) has argued, "furniture embodies the unknown but resurgent past" (p. 10) as "past acts lie petrified in household objects" and the habitats within which the characters are framed "bear a sinister resemblance to crypts or mausoleums," which are, moreover, "always 'pre-inhabited' . . . their living inmates find themselves hemmed in by other people's things, which are imbued with secrets of preceding generations . . . passions . . . inhere in furniture long after their human performers have departed" (p. 9).

HOUSE, NOVEL, PSYCHE

Changes in houses reflect changes in emotional states and vice versa, as the fixed material forms of domestic spaces mirror and shape the fluid immaterial self. According to Bachelard (1994: xxxvii), Carl Jung's conceptualization of domestic structures, both architectural and literary, as replications or images of mental structures, offered grounds for "taking the house as a tool for analysis of the human soul."[15] While Bachelard's *The Poetics of Space* continues to provide invaluable insights into the symbolism of home, in its unproblematic benignity, it stops short of investigating the role home plays in Freudian psychoanalysis. And it is precisely to Freud that Rachel Bowlby (1995: 77) turns to critique Bachelard's romanticization of the ideal childhood home, which finds no room for the *unheimlich*. As she argues, "in psychoanalysis the home is no place of harmony:" "[t]he house . . . is irredeemably driven by the presence of ghosts, its comforting appearance of womblike unity doubled from the start by intruding forces . . . untimely and dislocated hauntings of other times and places and other presences."

If, in comparable and repetitive ways, novels and houses—as structures, constructs, shelters, built forms—endeavor to make sense of the world, to imagine and create ways of being at home in a world where we do not feel at home, they attempt to represent and reckon with the unhomely and with the possibility that a return to the intimacy of "le toutounier" may be also oppressive and stifling.

Freud's investigation of the coincidence of homely and unhomely and his insight into the disturbing slipperiness of the familiar is particularly useful in understanding the role of those uncanny sites—cellars, dungeons, attics, overgrown gardens—that are so ubiquitous in the Gothic novel, an excessive, nightmarish permutation of the domestic novel. The Gothic, haunted by the specter of father-daughter incest, flourished during the eighteenth century, precisely the period that saw the emergence of the nuclear family with its attendant intimacy and privacy. The horror of domestic interment/disinterment, so pervasive in the Gothic, is also apparent in the work of nineteenth and twentieth century writers and literary critics, from E. T. A. Hoffmann to Henry James, as well as in the "unhomely" houses of Dada and surrealism. The "interuterine" houses imagined by Tristan Tzara, the soluble habitations delineated by Dali, the "soft" houses of Matta offer ready examples (Vidler 1995–2000: 71). Following this lead, a long tradition of feminist work has pursued the disruption of the resonances of tranquillity so usually associated with home and has exposed the home as the site of exploitation, oppression, and violence (Massey 2000 [1995]: 41): "home, in a sense, has always been *unheimlich*, unhomely; not just the utopian place of safety and shelter for which we supposedly yearn, but also the place of dark secrets, of fear and danger, that we can sometimes only inhabit furtively"(Bammer 1992: xi). One only needs to think of recent installations like Rachel Whiteread's "House" and her casts of basic objects of urgent daily use, nagged and stained by wear and tear, or Louise Bourgeois's "cells," evocative of inclusion and exclusion, vulnerability and protection, to realize the compelling suggestiveness of such reciprocity. In Whiteread's "House" the complete sealing off of the interior, far from suggesting safety and protection, "argued for the necessity of burying the familiar and the familial, of preventing the escape of dark forces, psychic toxins," while Bourgeois's work, stemming from "the same Viennese culture in which Freud developed his theories" provides an antithesis to Bachelard's idealization of childhood and an extensive and vivid commentary on the family as source of trauma (Mengham 2000: 41, 42). In E. M. Delafield's *Nothing is Safe* (1937) it is the divorce of the parents that shatters Julia's and Terry's world. A number of domestic novels, however, in a curious harking back to the pervasive figure of the live burial of uncompliant daughters in Gothic fiction, present modern versions of the young heroine buried alive. In Delafield's earlier novel, *Consequences* (2000 [1919]), Alex Clare's wilfulness and strongheadedness as a child is crushed when she reaches the age for "coming out" and must submit to the family's pressure to find a suitable husband. Feeling at variance with her surroundings, unable to settle either for marriage with a simple, egotistic young man or with the life as a nun that she has mistakenly chosen as a refuge, she will end up drowning herself. Mary Olivier in the eponymous novel and Joan Ogden in *The Unlit Lamp* are casebook examples of lives strangulated by the tyranny of the family (the working title of *The Unlit Lamp* had been "Octopi") (Joannou 1995: 80).

EVERYDAY AND DOMESTIC RITUALS, OR *PARVA, SI NON FIANT QUOTIDIE*[16]

Domestic space, however, implies more than houses and gardens, or liminal spaces of staircase, garden gate, doorstep, porch, garage, and their archetypical, Freudian, anthropomorphic, embodied or ontological significance. It implies the everyday, the rituals of domesticity in their cyclical, repetitive ordinariness—home culture. E. M. Delafield's *Diary of a Provincial Lady* (1984 [1930]), Jan Struther's *Mrs Miniver* (1989 [1939]), Elizabeth Bowen's *The Death of the Heart* (1938), Enid Bagnold's *The Squire* (1987 [1938]), Lettice Cooper's *The New House* (1987 [1936]) articulate a kind of epistemology of the home and interpret their being in the world through domestic ritual and the language of the everyday.[17] While in 1909 Cicely Hamilton had noted with displeasure that even that most feminine of occupations, maternity, had always been treated by women "in exactly the same spirit in which it is commonly handled by men from the superficial point of view of the outsider, the person who has no actual experience of the subject (Hamilton 1909: 113), by the 1920s and 1930s domestic novelists had begun to view the world, family, the house from inside the domestic sphere through the lens of housework, housekeeping, cooking, cleaning, decorating. By means of this grammar of the house, they imposed order upon the disorder of living, thus exploring what E. H. Young (1990 [1937]: 16) called "the art of living." Hence, in Betty Miller's *Farewell Leicester Square* (2000 [1941]), it is precisely the focus on the reiteration of tasks such as dusting, polishing, the patient unraveling every morning of stale sheets and blankets that in a rare moment of tenderness illumines the figure of Mrs Berman: her hands, "roughened from the ceaseless régime of housework" are the "hands of an artist, in the nearest sense creative" (p. 13). As Rita Felski (1999–2000: 20) has persuasively argued in her defense of the temporal rhythms of everyday life, "[r]epetition, understood as ritual . . . situates the individual in an imagined community that spans historical time. It is thus not opposed to transcendence, but it is the means of transcending one's historically limited existence." Perhaps tongue-in-cheek Carol Shields (2000: 40), arguably the most talented follower of the English domestic novelists, hints at the same when she has a character compare her daily chores to the rituals of Buddhist monks, who "devote two hours to morning meditation, followed by one hour of serious cleaning. Saffron-robed and their shaved heads gleaming, they actually go out into the world each day with buckets and rags, and they clean . . . anything that needs cleaning, a wall or an old fence, whatever presents threat or disorder."

Even though, as Jeannette Bertz Cooperman (1999) notes in her study of domesticity and post-feminist novels, *The Broom Closet*, "housework does not always reach the communicative and performative level of ritual," "[p]erforming ritual . . . not only reminds us of an underlying cosmic order, it helps establish that order" (Cooperman, quoting Driver, 1999: 5). "Like housework, it is deliberately repetitive, thus denying the passage of time and the fearfulness of change" (p. 5). The ghostly repetition and return of domestic rituals—the gathering at the breakfast table, which begins so many novels, the retreat to the study, and the interruption of tea—shape the narratives of the inter-war domestic novel. Ivy Compton-Burnett's study of patriarchal tyranny, *A House and its Head* (1958 [1935]), opens with an unpleasant family breakfast scene; subsequent breakfasts are haunted by the ghosts of a recently deceased mother and wife, an adulterous and runaway wife, and infanticide. Compton-Burnett even has her characters repeat the same words in the recurring breakfast scenes. In *School for Spinsters*, the tyranny of the tea ritual is such that a mother's death will be announced over "a slice of walnut cake" (Pertwee 1948: 28). Like the ancestral home, domestic ritual both shelters and nurtures the self and imagination, yet also stifles and oppresses individuality.

DOMESTICITY AND/OR MODERNITY

While the everyday would seem to place the domestic novel within the tradition of realism (Langbauer 1999: 2), the investment in the representation of the everyday of modernist writers committed to literary experimentation, such as Virginia Woolf and Katherine Mansfield, reminds us that the everyday and the domestic played a complicated role in the evolution of high modernism. Christopher Reed's (1996: 16) claim that "[t]he domestic, perpetually invoked in order to be denied, remains throughout the course of modernism a crucial site of anxiety and subversion" is central to our reading of English inter-war domestic novels and to our argument that, far from being inherently conservative politically and technically this genre was essentially a discourse of opposition—one that haunted high modernism. Uncannily, the very words that Freud used to describe the field of exploration of psychoanalysis aptly describe the concern of the domestic novel: "the material for its [psychoanalysis'] observations is usually provided by the inconsiderable events which have been put aside by the other sciences as being too unimportant—the dregs, one might say, of the world of phenomena . . . the idea of the unconscious as something that is both everywhere and nowhere offers a compelling analogy for the everyday" (Freud 1974: 52, quoted in Highmore 2002).

Though obscured by the flamboyant experiments of the high modernists, the domestic novel of the inter-war years was well attuned to the exigencies of modernity. The domestic novelists, so often accused of harboring reactionary feelings of nostalgia for a more stable society, were on the contrary joining efforts with modern phenomena such as Mass Observation and the Documentary Film Movement in the 1930s in rendering vivid the everyday—the drama of the doorstep—"without its everydayness being remaindered" (Highmore 2002: 39). Like Mass Observation and the Documentary Film Movement, inter-war domestic novelists faced the challenge of finding forms to rescue moments that have been too often considered too transitory to catch the eye. This was no easy task; for, though as Lefebvre famously pointed out," [c]ulture can no longer be conceived outside the everyday," the special quality of the everyday may indeed be "its lack of quality. It might be precisely the unnoticed, the unconspicuous, the unobtrusive" (Highmore 2002: 1), what Carol Shields calls "the mucilage of daily life that cements our genuine moments of being . . . accumulating at the side of the story but not claiming any importance for itself." (Shields 2002: 64)."

THE (RE)TURN TO DOMESTIC SPACE

> Looking round Number 9 Taraline Street, one is struck by its supreme inconvenience. It was designed by men architects, and men don't live and move and have their being in their houses (Eyles 1922).

In the inter-war years the domestic space is solely constructed by men; thus in architectural discourse domestic space predictably suffers from being the disadvantaged term in a series of gendered binaries which inform and structure architectural thinking and building. Feminist architects and architectural historians, however, have begun to revalue the importance of the home and its occupants with particular attention to women's experience and role in consumption and production. Along with feminist geographers, historians, and anthropologists they have contributed to an understanding of how home and house are gendered and femininized in garden cities, suburban villas, and council housing (Mezei and Briganti 2002b). For some, this turn to domestic space and the domestic interior was a trap, but for others, a haunt of privacy and Bachelardian dreaming, microcosmic worlds in which to experience the art of living. Thus, the narrator of E. H. Young's *Celia*, reflects:

> Celia's was a narrow world, but what more was the greater world
> than a container of personalities and the pain and happiness

they could bestow on their fellows. Here, in little were most of the emotions, preoccupations and duties common to man-kind—love, dislike, anxiety and doubt and the perpetual problem of right and wrong (Young 1990 [1937]: 225–6).

In *Mary Olivier*, Mary, despite or perhaps because of the constraints of her quiet narrow domestic world, becomes a successful poet (Sinclair 1919), while in *To the Lighthouse* Lily Briscoe, another spinster, who lives a quiet life with her father in London, paints post-impressionistic canvases.

The effort to study and validate domestic life parallels a resurgence and revaluation of the domestic novel and of novelists who have been traditionally marginalized because of their focus on that which has accumulated at the side of the story, the unnoticed, the inconspicuous, the unobtrusive. In their turn to domestic space and the domestic interior, domestic novelists of the inter-war years inaugurated a turn to interiority, feminine subjectivity and the everyday, thus privileging the private and the ordinary and the lives of middle-class women and a new haunting of house and novel.

NOTES

1. This article is an expanded and substantially revised version of our "Hanté par les maisons: l'espace domestique et roman domestique anglais," *Espaces domestiques: construire, aménager, répresenter,* eds Béatrice Collignon and Jean-François Staszak. Paris: Bréal, 2003. We acknowledge and thank Béatrice Collignon, Jean-François Staszak, and Bréal Press.
2. As we are wary of the pitfalls of stringent periodization, we have given ourselves permission to include in our study texts that trespass the strict chronological frame of the inter-war years.
3. This concerted advocation of a return to the home has been well documented. Cf. Beddoe 1989, Chapman and Hockey (1999), Giles (1995), Humble (2001) and Trodd (1998).
4. This articulation emerged out of astute comments by Jean-François Staszak and Elsa Ramos during the Espaces Domestiques conference, Paris, 2002, for which we thank them.
5. As its Latin source (*domesticus*; *domus*) suggests, "domestic" signifies of/or belonging to the home, house or household; accordingly, the English domestic novel, which sets the model for the genre in other literatures in English, portrays the social relations and daily life of a contained community—house, village, urban parish. Domestic novels, particularly during the inter-war years in the twentieth century, depict bourgeois family life, domestic rituals and domestic spaces, most often through a woman's perspective. For a fuller definition, see Briganti and Mezei (1999: 197).
6. See Davidoff (1979: 64–97). In *Apartment Stories*, Sharon Marcus (1999) observes the difference between London and Paris urban

architecture, noting that while Parisians lived in apartment buildings, Londoners, caught up in a rural beau ideal of the home, resorted to lodgings in private homes—rooms, bedsits, garden flats. See also Davidoff *et al.* (1976: 139–75) and Ford (1988).

7. In *Desire and Domestic Fiction: A Political History of the Novel*, Nancy Armstrong (1987: 3) observes that "domestic fiction . . . emerged with the rise of the domestic woman and established its hold over British culture through her dominance over all those objects and practices we associate with private life."

8. See the "Complete list of all Penguin and Pelican Books to the end of 1938" appended to Seymour (1938 [1928]).

9. From November 1 2003, Design Museum, London (www.designmuseum.org).

10. Coincidentally, Allen Lane conceived the idea of a good quality paperback, which would only cost the price of a pack of cigarettes, when returning to London after a weekend at the Devon home of Agatha Christie; waiting for a train at the Exeter station and seeking something to read, he found only reprints of nineteenth-century novels. In a further coincidence, Christie lived in the Lawn Road Flats, which she famously compared to a giant ocean liner without any funnels, from 1940 to 1946 at No. 22. The Lawn Road Flats in North London were built by a Canadian architect, Wells Coates, for Isokon, the design firm, founded by Molly and Jack Pritchard, known for plywood furniture. The concept was bauhaus, sleek, modern, urban, organic, minimalist; there was a communal restaurant, the Isobar, and residents included Walter Gropius, Marcel Breuer and Lazslo Molnar-Nagy.

11. For a fuller list of women's magazines that appeared in the interwar years, see White (1970: 95–6, 312–15). See also Beetham (1996).

12. For the idea of the textualization of domestic space, we thank James Duncan.

13. In George Eliot's *Middlemarch* (1968 [1871–2]: 110), the young doctor Lydgate reflects on the French anatomist, Bichat in precisely these terms: "That great Frenchman first carried out the concept that living bodies . . . are not associations of organs which can be understood by studying them first apart, and then, as it were, federally; but must be regarded as consisting of certain primary webs or tissues, out of which the various organs—brain, heart, lungs, and so on—are compacted, as the various accommodations of a house are built up in various proportions of wood, iron, stone, brick, zinc, and the rest, each material having its peculiar composition and proportions . . ."[11]

14. Quoted in Judy Collins and Sophie Howarth's display caption for Edouard Vuillard's "Jeune femme dans un intérieur" (1910) in the permanent collection of Tate Modern, London.

15. See also Clare Cooper Marcus (1995).

16. "Matters that one would call trivial if they were not part of a daily routine" (Pliny 1965: 37).

17. We are, of course, indebted to Sedgwick's *Epistemology of the Closet* (1990).

REFERENCES

Armstrong, Nancy. 1987. *Desire and Domestic Fiction: A Political History of the Novel*. New York: Oxford University Press.

Bachelard, Gaston. 1994. *The Poetics of Space*. Trans. Maria Jolas. Boston, MA: Beacon Press.

Bagnold, Enid. 1987 [1938]. *The Squire*. London: Virago.

Bammer, Angelika. 1992. "Editorial: The Question of 'Home.'" *New Formations* 17: vii–xi.

Beauman, Nicola. 1983. *A Very Great Profession: The Woman's Novel 1914–1939*. London: Virago.

Beddoe, Deirdre. 1989. *Back to Home and Duty: Women Between the Wars 1918–1939*. London: Pandora.

Beetham. Margaret. 1996. *A Magazine of Her Own: Domesticity and Desire in the Woman's Magazine. 1800–1914*. London: Routledge.

Bhabha, Homi. 1997. "The World and the Home." In Anne McClintock, Aamir Mufti, and Ella Shohat (eds) *Dangerous Liaisons: Gender, Nation and Postcolonial Perspectives*, pp. 445–55. Minneapolis MN: University of Minneapolis Press.

Bird, Jon. 2000 [1995]. "Dolce Domum." In James Lingwood (ed.) *House*, pp. 110–25. London: Phaidon.

Bowlby, Rachel. 1995. "Domestication." in D. Elam and R. Wiegman (eds) *Feminism Beside Itself*, pp. 71–91. London: Routledge.

Bowen, Elizabeth. 1938. *The Death of the Heart*. New York: Knopf.

——. 1960 [1948]. *The Heat of the Day*. New York: Knopf.

——. 1979 [1929]. *The Last September*. New York: Avon Books.

——. 1980. "The New House." *The Collected Stories of Elizabeth Bowen*. London: Jonathan Cape.

Bourdieu, Pierre. 1990. *The Logic of Practice*. Trans. Richard Nice. Cambridge: Polity Press.

Brittain, Vera. 1930. "Why I Think Mothers Can Have Careers." *Good Housekeeping* XVIII(2): 55, 146–8.

Burnett, John. 1986. *A Social History of Housing: 1815–1985*. London: Methuen.

Carsten, Janet and Hugh-Jones, Stephen (eds) 1995. "Introduction." *About the House—Lévi-Strauss and Beyond* pp. 1–21. Cambridge: Cambridge University Press.

Chapman, Tony, and Hockey, Jenny (eds) 1999. "The Ideal Home as it is Imagined and as it is Lived." *Ideal Homes? Social Change and Domestic Life*, pp. 1–13. London: Routledge.

Colette (Sidonie Gabrielle). 1939. *Le Toutounier*. Paris: Frenczi.

Compton-Burnett, Ivy. 1958 [1935]. *A House and its Head*. Harmondsworth: Penguin.

Cooper, Lettice. 1987 [1936]. *The New House*, London: Virago.

Cooperman, Jeannette B. 1999. *The Broom Closet: Secret Meanings of Domesticity in Postfeminist Novels by Louise Edrich, Mary Gordon, Toni Morrison, Marge Piercy, Jane Smiley, and Amy Tan*. New York: Peter Lang.

Davidoff, Leonore. 1979. "The Separation of Home and Work? Landladies and Lodgers in Nineteenth- and Twentieth-Century England." In Sandra Burman (ed.) *Fit Work for Women*, pp. 64–97. London: Croom Helm.

Davidoff, Leonore, Jean L'Esperance and Howard Newby. 1976. "Landscape with Figures: Home and Community in English Society." In Juliet Mitchell and Ann Oakley (eds) *The Rights and Wrongs of Women*, pp. 139–75. Harmondsworth: Penguin.

Delafield, E.M. 1937. *Nothing is Safe*. New York, Harper.

——. 1984 [1930]. *The Diary of a Provincial Lady*. London: Virago.

——. 1989 [1932]. *Thank Heaven Fasting*. London: Virago.

——. 2000 [1919]. *Consequences*. London: Persephone.

Derrida, Jacques. 1994. Specters of Marx: *The State of the Debt, the Work of Mourning, and the New International*. Trans. Peggy Kamuf. New York: Routledge.

du Maurier, Daphne. 1938. *Rebecca*. New York: Avon.

Ellmann, Maude. 2001. "Elizabeth Bowen: The Shadowy Fifth." In Rod Mengham and N. H. Reeve (eds) *The Fiction of the 1940s: Stories of Survival*, pp. 1–25. London: Palgrave.

Eliot, George. 1968 [1871–2]. *Middlemarch*. Cambridge, MA: Riverside.

Eyles, Leonora. 1922. *The Woman in the Little House*. London: Richards.

Felski, Rita. 1999–2000. "The Invention of Everyday Life." *New Formations* 39: 15–31.

Ford, Boris (ed.). 1988. *The Cambridge Guide to the Arts in Britain*. Cambridge; New York: Cambridge University Press.

Forster, E. M. 1970 [1910]. *Howards End*. Harmondsworth: Penguin.

Frank, Ellen Eva. 1979. *Literary Architecture: Essays Towards a Tradition, Walter Pater, Gerard Manley Hopkins, Marcel Proust, Henry James*. Berkeley, CA: University of California Press.

Freud, Sigmund. 1974. *Introductory Lectures on Psychoanalysis [1916–17]*. Trans. James Strachey. Harmondsworth: Penguin.

Garber, Marjorie. 2000. *Sex and Real Estate: Why We Love Houses*. New York: Pantheon.

Giles, Judy. 1995. *Women, Identity and Private Life in Britain, 1900–50*. London: Macmillan.

Hall, Radclyffe. 1981 [1924]. *The Unlit Lamp*. London: Virago.

——. 1959. "Fräulein Schwartz." In *Miss Ogilvy Finds Herself*, pp. 107–37. London: Hammond.

Hamilton, Cecily. 1909. *Marriage as a Trade*. London: Chapman.

Harbison, Robert. 2000. *Eccentric Spaces*. Cambridge, MA: MIT Press.

Highmore, Ben. 2002. *Everyday Life and Cultural Theory: An Introduction*. London: Routledge.

Humble, Nicola. 2001. *The Feminine Middlebrow Novel, 1920s–1950s: Class, Domesticity, and Bohemianism*. Oxford: Oxford University Press.

Jameson, Storm. 1926. *Three Kingdoms*. London: Constable.

——. 1927. "Marriage—The Most Difficult Profession in the World." *Good Housekeeping* XI(4): 16–17, 105–6.

Jameson, Frederic. 1999. "Is space Political?" In Neil Leach (ed.) *Rethinking Architecture: A Reader in Cultural Theory*, pp. 255–69. New York: Routledge.

Joannou, Maroula. 1995. *"Ladies, Please Don't Smash These Windows:" Women's Writing, Feminist Consciousness and Social Change 1918–38*. Oxford & Providence, RI: Berg.

Langbauer, Laurie. 1999. *Novels of Everyday Life: The Series in English Fiction, 1850–1930*. Ithaca: Cornell University Press.

Lehmann, Rosamund. 1982 [1930]. *A Note in Music*. London: Virago.

Leverson, Ada. 1982 [1908–16]. *The Little Ottleys*. London: Virago.

Lyotard, Jean-François. 1999. "*Domus* and the Megalopolis." In Neil Leach (ed.) *Rethinking Architecture: A Reader in Cultural Theory*. London: Routledge.

Macaulay, Rose. 1967 [1926]. *Crewe Train*. London: Collins.

Marcus, Clare Cooper. 1995. *House as a Mirror of Self*. Berkeley, CA: Conari.

Marcus, Sharon. 1999. *Apartment Stories: City and Home in Nineteenth-Century Paris and London*. Berkeley, CA: University of California Press.

Massey, Doreen. 2000 [1995]. "Space-Time and the Politics of Location." In James Lingwood (ed.) *House*, pp. 34–49. London: Phaidon.

Mengham, Rod. 2000. "Innervisions." In Iwona Blazwick and Simon Wilson (eds) *Tate Modern Handbook*. London: Tate Publishing.

Mezei, Kathy and Chiara Briganti. 1999. "Domestic Novel." In Lorna Sage (ed.) *The Cambridge Guide to Women's Writing in English*, p. 197. Cambridge: Cambridge University Press.

——. 2002a. "Reading the House: A Literary Perspective." *Signs* 27(3): 837–46.

——. 2000b. "Forum: Domestic Space." *Signs* 27(3): 813–900.

Miller, Betty. 2000 [1941]. *Farewell Leicester Square*. London: Persephone.

Morley, David. 2000. *Home Territories: Media, Mobility and Identity*. London: Routledge.

O'Shea, Prudence. 1932. "The Happiest Way of Things." *Good Housekeeping* XXI(3): 54–5, 144, 146–7.

Panter-Downes, Mollie. 1985 [1947]. *One Fine Day*. London: Virago.

Pertwee, Roland. 1948. *School for Spinsters: A Comedy in Three Acts*. English Theatre Guild Ltd.

Pliny. 1965. *Selected Letters of Pliny,* III.1. Introduction and Notes by J. H. Westcott. Norman, OH: University of Oklahoma Press.

Reed, Christopher. 1996. "Introduction." *Not at Home: The Suppression of Domesticity in Modern Art and Architecture*, pp. 7–17. London: Thames and Hudson.

Robertson, E. Arnot. 1989 [1928]. *Cullum*. London: Virago.

Rybczynski, Witold. 1986. *Home: A Short History of An Idea*. New York: Viking.

Sedgwick, Eve Kosofsky. 1990. *Epistemology of the Closet*. Berkeley, CA: University of California Press.

Seymour, Beatrice Kean. 1938 [1928]. *Youth Rides Out*. Harmondsworth: Penguin.

Shields, Carol. 2002. *Unless*. London: Fourth Estate.

Shone, Richard. 2000. "A Cast in Time." In James Lingwood (ed.) *Rachel Whiteread's House*, pp. 50–61. London: Phaidon.

Sidlauskas, Susan. 1996. "Psyche and Sympathy: Staging Interiority in the Early Modern Home." In Christopher Reed (ed.) *Not at Home*, pp. 65–80. London: Thames and Hudson.

Sinclair, May. 1919. *Mary Olivier: A Life*. New York: Macmillan.

Smith, Dodie. 1976 [1948]. *I Capture the Castle*. New York: St Martin's Griffin.

Struther, Jan. 1989 [1939]. *Mrs Miniver*. London: Virago.

Tristram, Philippa. 1989. *Living Space in Fact and Fiction*. London: Routledge.

Trodd, Anthea. 1998. *Women's Writing in English: Britain 1900–1945*. Edinburgh: Longman.

Vidler, Anthony. 1995–2000. "A Dark Space." In James Lingwood (ed.) *Rachel Whiteread's House*, pp. 62–72. London: Phaidon.

Waugh, Evelyn. 1945. *Brideshead Revisited: The Sacred and Profane Memoirs of Captain Charles Ryder*. Boston, MA: Little, Brown.

West, Rebecca. 1980 [1929]. *Harriet Hume*. London: Virago.

White, Cynthia L. 1970. *Women's Magazines: 1693–1968*. London: Michael Joseph.

Wilson, Elizabeth. 1991. *The Sphinx in the City: Urban Life, the Control of Disorder, and Women*. London: Virago.

Woolf, Virginia. 1928. "Introduction to Mrs Dalloway." In *Mrs Dalloway*, pp. 25–37. New York: Modern Library Edition.

——. 1970 [1941]. *Between the Acts*. San Diego: Harcourt.

——. 1994 [1927]. *To the Lighthouse*. London, New York: Routledge.

Young, E. H. 1916. *Moor Fires*. London: John Murray.

——. 1947. *Chatterton Square*. London: Cape.

——. 1988 [1925]. *William*. London: Virago.

——. 1990 [1937]. *Celia*. London: Virago.

——. 1985 [1932]. Jenny Wren. London: Virago.

HOME CULTURES   VOLUME 1, ISSUE 2.   REPRINTS AVAILABLE   PHOTOCOPYING   © BERG 2004
PP 169–186   DIRECTLY FROM THE   PERMITTED BY LICENSE   PRINTED IN THE UK
PUBLISHERS.   ONLY

RUSSELL HITCHINGS
AT HOME WITH SOMEONE NONHUMAN

RUSSELL HITCHINGS IS DOING A PHD IN HUMAN GEOGRAPHY AT UNIVERSITY COLLEGE LONDON. THIS PROJECT CONCERNS THE EVERYDAY SPACE OF THE PRIVATE DOMESTIC GARDEN IN CONTEMPORARY LONDON AND EXAMINES THE CHANGING WAYS IN WHICH PEOPLE AND PLANTS LIVE TOGETHER THERE.

This article explores some new theoretical ground to reveal the many intentions at play within the home. Specifically, I am interested in intentions that are not always reducible to the human agency of the people that dwell there. Whilst we may imaginatively think that we are safe and in charge of the things surrounding us at home, all sorts of forces may be at work there, obscured, in part, by both academic and non-academic considerations. This article traces some elements of a science-studies approach to the network of many different jostling actors in the home space. Through reconsidering the natural scientist's approach to agency and the capacity of entities to object to what we say about them, it is possible to enliven a currently prevalent anthropological stance on home material cultures. From this vantage, we can productively expand the notion of home lives and reveal how things in the domestic are always less than fully domesticated.

INTRODUCTION: ON HEATING SYSTEMS AND MOORLAND STONECROPS

In the early 1990s, the British government launched a campaign to promote more sustainable domestic energy use, arguing that "helping the earth begins at home" (see Hinchliffe 1997). Within a context of an individualized politics advocated by the contemporary administration, the argument went that if society wanted a more sustainable future, then getting there was the responsibility of everyone, and everyone should, therefore, think about the ways in which their daily routines at home impacted upon the global environment. However, this campaign, together with a wider approach to individual responsibility in sustainable living (on this see Burgess *et al.* 2003), proved largely unsuccessful. Through an in-depth study of domestic energy use in Bristol, Hinchliffe suggests one of the main reasons for this failure was that the politics of reconnection enshrined in such a campaign was simply too ambitious. Notions of power generation, natural resources, and environmental damage seemed simply too far removed from people's daily experiences of the home, which serves, imaginatively at least, as an "ontologically secure" (Hinchliffe 1997: 201) place of social intimacy and retreat from such external forces and issues. The home is, as he and others (see Clarke 2001) have suggested, perceived as an "ideal home" and an intimate conversation with an idealized self. From this vantage, it is a refuge from the world, a place of our own of which we are in charge, and this ontological stability is too forcefully imagined for the home to become an end point in a chain of transforming natural resources. Indeed this might equally stand for external agencies more generally. Like the city and the country (Williams 1973), the home and the environment, here, seem mutually exclusive, symbolically at least.

From this perspective, the home is a space for humans in the imagination of the people dwelling within. Certainly it is not a place where the natural world has much presence. The home space is a domestic space and, by implication, things there would be domesticated. A focus upon human control within a personal refuge from the world seems to be a collorary of an idea of home. However, whilst this was the perspective taken by Hinchliffe's Bristol respondents, it is clearly not the only way of approaching the issues at stake. The officials behind the government campaign would perhaps ruefully remind us that we could also connect the home to other places and alien forces. For me, here, this is a useful reminder.

Like the heating systems in the homes of Bristol, the peculiar rock formations on the hills of Bodmin Moor can be thought about in different ways. For Tilley *et al.* (2000) what is particularly interesting are the "clitter" stones there: the array of smaller stones that can be found around the tors and settlements of these Bronze Age sites. These stones have been largely overlooked, in favor of such larger relics, in past archaeological analysis, yet, they suggest, they might productively be further explored. These stones could be written about in a number of ways. As Law and Singleton (2000) would argue, these stones could be differentially "performed," according to our different academic disciplinary "modes of ordering" (Law 1994). If we look at them in the way that a natural scientist traditionally has, we would see a dynamic landscape moved through processes of solifluction, frost heave, and rockfall with the passage of time and natural erosion. If we look at them in the way a cultural archaeologist would, they could, however, also become circular arrangements of cultural landscape and symbolic appropriation, as markers of significance to the Bronze Age peoples that lived with them. These mysterious stones can take on different meanings, then, according to the academic perspective that is adopted. Their agency might lie with the natural world or with the social world. We could perhaps think of them as being rooted in both at once. Through an oscillation between different disciplinary framings of their agency, they suggest, we could develop a richer phenomenological understanding of these stones and a richer understanding of how the Bronze Age settlers might themselves have encountered them in ritualistic practice, as conduits both to other groups and also to more mysterious other worlds (Tilley *et al.*, 2000). The sources of their agency might have been more open for the ancient settlers living with them, and not as tied down as they might be now within different academic disciplines, and, in this, these settlers provide me with another useful reminder.

It is with these two contrasting stories that I want to begin this article about agency within the home. The point of the first is to suggest that we perhaps do not want to think about nonhuman agencies making their way into the home or, at least, that we are not used to doing so. The point of the second is to recognize that we could think about the world in all sorts of ways, if we mixed up and opened out our academic frames of reference. Together they offer a useful starting point.

Academic frames serve to order the world to the implicit benefit of certain perspectives just like people do in their home lives. Yet, if we were to explore the agencies of the home in some other ways, we could provide some different insight. As with the clitter stones, a richer picture might emerge through exploring and expanding the theoretical perspectives brought to bear on a particular place. In studies of the home my argument here is that the array of agencies at work there might be currently downplayed, and that this situation could be complemented by a exploration of some other approaches that I want to outline. In a similar format to the ways in which a new approach offered new meaning to the clitter stones—in this case the addition of more phenomenological social methods to traditional natural science—so this could also apply to the study of the home space—in this case through an expansion of traditionally social interpretations towards the natural sciences. Certain academic perspectives may have been like the Bristol homeowners in the way in which they have tended to focus on the social lives of homes. Yet what we could also look for are some of the other creative presences (Whatmore 2002) that dwell there. Our home spaces could be like the clitter stones if we wanted them to be. Natural agency, as well as social agency, could potentially be found there.

Such is the argument that I want to make in this article. First, however, I want to review how home materials have already been considered. I want to explore where some current approaches take us before starting at an alternative point. This alternative point begins with some developments in science studies and, using these particular insights, I then want to explore how we could recast the home and the many lives within it. Currently anthropologists seem to hold sway over research into home material cultures and they have revealed a certain type of anthropological understanding. What an approach from science studies can offer is an alertness to the ways in which the objects of the home can object to what is said about them and reveal how finding meaning within things at home can involve an unstable performance of many different agencies.

HOW THINGS CAN MATTER IN THE HOME SPACE

Within the social sciences, approaches to the materials that comprise domestic environments have been most well developed with cultural anthropology. This is hardly surprising for a number of reasons that can be associated with the specific concerns of this discipline.

Anthropologists, for instance, have, traditionally at least, tended to go to unfamiliar places and research daily life and culture there. On arrival, the strangeness of the materials of the home would have been evident from the outset, as would be their unfamiliar role in the structuring and maintenance of these cultures. These objects would be alien to the researcher and be used in unfamiliar ways. Therefore, they would be more immediately, and recognizably, of interest. Other social scientists traditionally worked within their own cultural groups, where the present material culture is more familiar and less remarkable. The researcher, therefore, might have felt less of a need to respond to it and so anthropologists have been the social scientists most likely to make drawings, to record physical matter, its arrangement, and its significance.

There is also the ethnographic method that is the cornerstone of the anthropological approach in its argument for a protracted period of direct physical intimacy with the subjects being studied. If a degree of time is spent within a cultural group, it might become, once again, hard to ignore the practical role of objects and artifacts in the reproduction of those structures. Other social sciences, meanwhile, with their interview methods and textual analyses have tended to implicitly privilege language and communication, as though the world was brokered through conversation and writing alone, such that the material assistance of objects and entities in the management of life might have seemed negligible.

There is, finally, also the professed agnosticism of the anthropological discipline in so far as a determinedly open stance is taken to the events unfolding around the researcher. The aim here is to minimize the degree of organizing structure brought to bear on the material the researcher is generating until a later point, when a set of wide-ranging notes are finally written up. With this aim in mind, the role of materials in structuring home lives has been allowed more of a place within anthropological accounts, both of these traditionally unfamiliar settings and also when this approach was taken to an anthropology "at home."

Consequently, as Tim Dant argues (1999: 8), anthropology has a head start in terms of exploring the ways and means by which we come to interact and make sense of the objects and entities that surround us. There is now a whole raft of material culture studies that explore such issues and, particularly, how such issues are played out in the home space since the home, within the ever-more privatized Western world at least, is increasingly the site where cultural reproductions are made and personal narratives take shape (Miller 2001a).

However, it is also important to consider the ways in which this specific discipline implicitly "orders" (Law 1994) the world. Despite a professed agnosticism, there are ways in which these anthropological studies do tend to structure the reality that they are presented with. For instance, some sort of denial of the fleeting nature of things is both a methodological necessity and a disciplinary project in anthropological orderings.

It is a methodological necessity in the sense that the method of anthropology is often a lengthy ethnographic engagement, and this method tends to lead to conclusions about static, deep, often hidden meanings. To produce conclusions about the ephemerality of the meaning of an object of material culture would go against the purpose of the method. The researcher would have spent years in a situation only to say that this situation no longer exists.

It is a disciplinary project in the way that Miller (1998b) suggests that the anthropology of material culture is about engaging with what "matters." This is an argument about engaging with what is important, as it is important to the people being studied, rather than what is important as it is important to current academic debates and this is a worthy project. However, he also argues that anthropology is about "uncovering" the importance of what is being presented, so that a particular idea about what something is *really* about emerges. There still seems to be a certain category of a deeper and, consequently, more docile, meaning that anthropology sees as its own territory. As Buchli (1999: 6) argues elsewhere, anthropology, and the anthropology of the home, can be criticized for a "prevailing preoccupation with the ethnographic and synchronic moment."

Within material culture research, the material is also, perhaps unsurprisingly, seen as the embodiment of the cultural. Miller (1995) again has argued that consumption could potentially replace kinship as the central concern of the anthropological discipline. This is because social relations can increasingly be seen to be constituted through the operation of commodities within consumption practices as much as through more human interactions within cultural groups (see also Douglas and Isherwood 1979). Within such a project, material culture is about cultural operation much more than about direct materiality. It is about how things like products, personal effects, or provisions serve to fulfill a cultural role. It is not about how products can wear out, how personal effects might need cleaning, or about how provisions might go off in the fridge. This particular sort of materiality is not as present as it might be.

In a recent article on the house in material culture studies, Miller (2001b) moves some way towards the type of issue that this article seeks to explore. He suggests there have been two dominant perspectives upon the house in past material culture research. It has either been considered as an expression of the agency of those that live within it (e.g. Clarke 1998), or as a cultural form held within a set of social power relations (e.g. Zukin 1991). What has been less considered is its direct materiality. This he explores through the idea of the "haunted" house, where the house can affect the owner in some more immediate ways. An attractive historic house can, for instance, remind the owner of his own inability to match the surrounding grandeur in terms of how the house is furnished. The house can therefore have agency. But this is a certain kind of agency. Miller draws upon Gell's "Art and Agency" (1998) to ground his account of these hauntings. For Gell, art can directly seduce the viewer and this is its agency. However, an anthropological mode of ordering still lingers within this engagement. Both the house and the work of art might affect us directly, but this effect is a product of past human activity—the effect of the architect or of the artist. This material agency still serves as an intermediary between humans. Rather than an intermediary between humans living together in the workings of culture, this is now an intermediary between temporally divided humans in the passage of history. Gell (1998: 8) admits the agency that concerns him is essentially human within an anthropological focus on social relations. We are not talking about how the house collects dust or how the painting needs varnishing. This would be a different kind of material agency. Here, we remain very much within the human sphere.

These developments feed into a broader shift within social science, where it is increasingly argued that the legacy of post-structuralist concerns for the relationality of meaning within language has too long precluded a more thorough consideration of the very bits and pieces with which cultural life is conducted (see Jackson 2000). That is to say that a concern for the representational and textual aspects of life has obscured the more practical encounters that are also essential to it. Within the home space, Miller suggests that the house has been understood as a social rather than a physical entity—discursively ordered through symbolic human meanings of home. This is "metaphor and not substance" (Miller 2001a: 12). Yet, whilst anthropologists have been at the forefront of attempts to grasp this substance, they have approached these entities in particular sorts of ways according to their disciplinary project. This has been, as I have argued, in a way that focuses on more static meanings and that strongly foregrounds the cultural relations between humans.

However, these materials might be examined otherwise. Like the clitter deposits on Bodmin moor, the things around us could be usefully written about from differing vantages. The home could be imaginatively a "purified" (Latour 1993) space—a space of culture, devoid of agencies other than those of the people that want to perceive themselves as in charge. Miller argues that we should approach material cultures that matter in the sense of being agnostic about how the things within people's lives can come to be important to them, but what of the matter of material culture in a more physical and visceral way? To explore such issues, one productive starting point, that I want to now outline, begins by stepping across the divide between social and natural sciences. This step may offer a new way of understanding the matters of our homes. If the potential liveliness of entities is, in part, obscured so far by an anthropological need to stabilize and reach for a certain sort of deeper meaning, this might not be the case elsewhere.

LIVING WITH OTHER MATTERS

The role of the social scientist, broadly, has been to explain things in relation to the social world, where answers were social ones and the things surrounding us embodied certain social functions. These accounts were ultimately about people and what people did. Yet, there may be other forces at play between people and things. Natural sciences, for instance, have a different agenda. The things around us in the world seem much livelier for the natural scientist. They make close observations of how things develop and change in certain places. Natural scientists monitor what certain things like and do not like to do by watching their behavior under their microscopes. Bacteria reproduce, but only in the conditions that they independently seem to like. Different animal populations expand and decline in areas of the world that are entirely uninhabited by humans. Vegetation covers develop over time as different species interact with each other to shape this development. All this could apparently happen without the intervention of people at all. Exploring the relations between the natural and the social sciences, and finding a place for this kind of agency within a more social account, has been a developing project within science studies that I want to now outline.

My account starts in the early 1980s and an apparent "social" turn in science studies. Here the practice of science was to be explored as a cultural and a historical activity as researchers no longer allowed science to sit as a separate field of endeavor, somehow standing aloof from the exchanges of social interaction that took place within all the other areas of human life. In this initial "strong project" (Bloor 1976), science was to be "socially constructed" and the power of the social was all important. Studies of science drew upon a contemporary linguistic focus within social research. Within this approach it was impossible for any object to exist independently of the signification practices surrounding it. What was actually hidden within a metaphor of scientific discovery was no more than a set of frantic representational maneuvers, either within society more generally, or within the conversations of the laboratory. Explanation now came from either a macro- or a micro-level appeal to social processes (Iseda 1998).

Macro-level historical studies would explore the effects of broad societal processes on scientific knowledge production. An example would be Shapin and Schaffer's (1989) study of Hobbes and Boyle in the seventeenth century. Their historical study could now conclude that Boyle's scientific work on air pressure was not only about the independent movement of molecules. Rather, it was also about public debate and the changing organization of society at the time he was working. It was these broader societal factors that made for a climate in which his claims could be publicly accepted, rather than these claims representing any sort of objective truth.

Micro-level studies examined the processes of knowledge production within science. A more ethnomethodological concern here (see for example Lynch 1993) was with the interactional achievements of the scientists themselves within their conversations. Lynch (1991), from this perspective, recognized that, when laboratory researchers describe the appearance of an object or measure it in some way, they do often employ specialized instruments and specific metric units in an attempt at replicable science. However, what he also argued was that their activities were not really contained within this disciplined stance. Description and measurement were also part of everyday life and what counted, as a sensible measurement, varied considerably from one context to another.

Whilst there were clearly a range of resources drawn upon, what remained the case here was that people became the central focus once again. Explicitly or implicitly, this area of research led to a denial of the agency of the natural entities that the scientists were trying to understand. Science was "constitutive" rather than "descriptive" of the things that it sought to identify (Knorr-Cetina 1981; Woolgar 1988). The natural world was to be treated as though "it did not affect our perception of it" (Collins 1983: 88). The object of study was, for them, almost a purely social thing once more. It was now no more than a passive pawn within a language game or the inert representation of a certain cultural formation. The natural world now had a small or non-existent role in this specifically "social" construction of science.

Whilst this initial approach seems to offer little for the aims of this article however, another strand within this field was beginning to allow the agency of things that were not human to force itself amongst the activities of the scientists that were seeking to render them knowable. Callon (1986) moved towards this approach in his description of science in action during a fishing dispute in the French bay of St Brieuc. Some scientists there had heard of a novel technique of scallop harvesting that had been experimented with in Japan. They thought that they could adapt this technique successfully for St. Brieuc. These scientists were, therefore, he argued, trying to speak on behalf of the scallops. They sought to represent how they would behave according to predictions based on a set of studies that other scientists had made of scallop activity. This they enshrined into their own scallop-harvesting technique. Yet, alas, the scallops did not behave in the way that the scientists suggested. They did not want to attach themselves to the specially designed harvesters. The scientific project collapsed.

This was a simple story, perhaps, but what Callon was theoretically doing here was developing a concept of "symmetrical" reconstruction, where the cause of scientific success or failure was attributed to a diffuse range of agents that were all treated equally in analysis. In this case they included fishermen, scallops, technologies, and scientists. Explanation was now not just about people in their social world, it was also about other entities within their supposedly natural world. They were all working together. Or not, as was the case in this instance.

Bruno Latour (1988) did something similar in an account of the achievements of Louis Pasteur in nineteenth-century France. Pasteur, he suggested, had to equally control both bacterial cultures and provincial farmers if he was to position himself as a successful scientist. Bacterial cultures needed an appropriate nutrient medium to grow in the Paris laboratory, just as provincial farmers needed persuasion that Pasteur could help them through some carefully staged public demonstrations. In this account, Pasteur is the central agent managing a precarious set of controlling activities. The progress of his scientific work was, therefore, the product of the activity of many things. His success and notoriety was not a consequence of any given genius of his own, but rather a result of the many different things working together in the process of sustaining the idea of this genius. This success was dependent upon a whole network of forces including the public hygiene movement, the medical profession, colonial interests and, tellingly, for this article, the actual bacteria and equipment he was handling within his experiments.

What these studies were asking was that if science could no longer be totally explained with reference to the operation of natural laws, why should we conversely assume that it might equally be totally explained with reference to social processes? What Latour asked for was "one more turn" after the "social turn" in science studies (Latour 1992), so that the world might better be understood as an operation of different kinds of entities working together. Large-scale systems in which scientific and technological artifacts come to be extended across time and space came through an idea of "enrolling" human and nonhuman elements within a set of "heterogeneous networks." Pasteur was enrolling farmers rhetorically, but also enrolling bacteria materially. Physical things now had a dynamic agency that was allowed a presence within a social-science narrative. These scientists were dealing with something lively in their attempts to organize themselves into the position of a provider of general truth. The scallops, the bacteria, and many other entities were now granted a mind of their own. They were sitting alongside the other human actors as unruly and lively things.

Work like that of Latour and of Callon came to be developed into a theoretical perspective that argued against structuring ontological positions. Such positions were now treated with skepticism from a position of determined close empiricism where things were allowed to do things, regardless of where they might have been previously classified. The researcher simply had to watch to see how and when different things interacted with each other within these networks of relationship and to watch for their effects. The exponents of this approach allowed the entities being studied to move between the static objects containing cultural and social meanings and the dynamic entities possessive of natural properties. Things were engaged with according to the ways in which they behaved, rather than according to a predefined set of ascribed categories and attributes that they were imagined to have possessed. Power and agency were not considered to be inherent within a particular thing simply because organizing lenses may have previously suggested that was where they lay.

There was a lot more helping constitute the social world from this vantage. Texts, technologies, people, and things were all taken to be significant within the performance of human life (Law 1994), and these ideas were initially carried forward into a number of new accounts of science and technology. Alcoholic liver disease, for instance, was no longer any kind of scientific condition in a traditional sense (Law and Singleton 2000). It was, rather, a notion that was constantly being recreated through the various different activities of any number of different entities. The structuring accounts of medical textbooks sought to inform a specific idea of this disease. The work practices of doctors made for certain accounts of its operation. The bodily operations of suggested sufferers would undermine or consolidate different understandings. They were all constitutive of the precarious performance of this particular disease.

In a reflective review of the relationship between social sciences and science studies, Latour (2000) considers what the social sciences might gain. What social studies have traditionally done, he argues, is to replace their object of inquiry with an idea of society. Society has been able to stand in as an explanatory principle for all things, so that the particularities of the things in question were lost. What we might rather do, he suggests, is find a way of productively emulating the natural sciences through a new conception of "objectivity." This objectivity is no longer to be considered negatively as a flawed attempt to deny human fallibility within natural scientific endeavor. It is, rather, thought of positively as the closest academic attempt that we have made to get in contact with the physical material presence of active entities. This objectivity is about an idea of making objections, since it is within the laboratory that scientists have given things the greatest opportunity to specifically object to what is said about them. It had been the earlier critiques of science-studies scholars that made the things being studied seem inert. What the social sciences have done, he suggests, is to imitate the natural sciences in a search for legitimacy. Consequently the locus of power became transferred from the thing being studied and the world of nature to the people that were studying and the world of society. However, they might imitate the natural scientist more productively in their conception of agency, since the last thing that a scientist would argue is that the microbes in the Petri dish or the enzymes in the tissue sample are completely passive.

From this viewpoint, all objects are now so specific that they cannot be replaced by something else for which they are supposed to be a stand-in. An object is not necessarily about an idea of culture and neither is it necessarily about an idea of nature. It is always a thing in its own right. What was allowed to happen was an "ontological choreography" (Cussins 1998) where the status of things was performed according to the specificity of the relations in which they operate. People could be subjects and objects, as could other things, according to the ways in which they interacted practically with each other in certain physical places. One example would be the way in which a car can become an office in the performance of mobile working (Laurier and Philo 1998). The job of the researcher was to explore these developments. In the expansion of a potential Paris transport network, Latour eventually allows the very train that was to run in this network an active voice within his account of these developments. The train finally asks the reader what exactly is a "self" and whether it might not be admitted within this category (Latour 1997), even though we might have been used to thinking of it as simply a train.

Entities, and the categories they were to belong to, were now in a process of flux and should be thought about in terms of "x-morphism" (see Laurier and Philo 1999),[1] where the frames of reference for understanding certain things would change according to context and where they were to always be allowed agency. From this vantage, we could be always living alongside someone nonhuman. The problem was just that we did not want to more fully recognize these presences. These theoretical developments made for a focus on an open and performative conception of the classification of an entity according to the properties it can be allowed to display within certain networks of association.

AT HOME WITH THE NONHUMANS

Such ideas from science studies have been used in a number of different contexts to develop narratives of evolving relationships between human and nonhuman allies. Principally, and unsurprisingly, these have been within more institutional and professional contexts since such contexts were not so far removed from the initial scientific environments where these ideas were developed and the human actors there, at least, also seemed to be discernibly working hard in the enrollment of the others around them. Yet my argument is that they can also be usefully used in the home space. Indeed, such ideas are now beginning to find their way there.

We might now productively think about the ways in which the practices of the home space are similar to the practices of science. We might want to think about how these insights about the ways in which actors interact are just as applicable to the living room as the nuclear laboratory (Shove 1999). In terms of technologies, Miller (1998a) has argued that grocery shopping might be about the demonstration of love within the home. Now, however, attention is drawn to how such demonstrations require work on the part of a variety of actors. To cook a loving meal, you would need an oven. You would need to know how to use that oven. You would have to have to time to wait for the meal to cook and something to put in the oven that would be happy to become something tasty. In short, it might only be possible to enact this love if the technological infrastructure and the organization of people and foods allowed the transformation of groceries into a loving meal. Technical objects like the fridge-freezer (Shove and Southerton 2000) can now be thought of as a demanding presence within contemporary human life, freezers have a "script" (Akrich 1992). They have certain expectations of the networks around them. Frozen-food stores must be relatively nearby. Electricity supply should be constant. There should also be a planned space for the freezer within the kitchen where it has gradually come to make its home. It also makes demands of the people that use it. They would have to learn that the freezer likes certain types of foods and not others. Maybe they would have to change their eating patterns accordingly. They also have to be ready to wait for the things that they give to the freezer to defrost again when the freezer hands it back to them. Through exploring this kind of freezer agency, this perspective has shown the many different changing activities that have gone into the creeping normalized expectations of the freezer as a taken-for-granted character within the average home. In 1970, 3% of British households owned at least one freezer. In 1995 this figure had risen to 96%. Such changes can now be productively explained as a product of concurrent developments situated simultaneously within symbolic meanings, practical infrastructures, and everyday practices and this may be a useful way of understanding the recent escalations of consumer expenditures within the context of an argument for sustainable living. Showers, equally (Hand *et al.* 2003), are active in orchestrating certain regimes of washing around them such that, once again, the material culture of the home can serve as a lively presence that promotes or constrains certain types of lifestyles and meaning, and certain sorts of patterns of, in this case intensifying, resource use.

Yet these technologies, whilst lively and demanding presences, are delegated to and, as such, could be thought of, once again, as akin to Gell's (1998) explicitly social agency since, as Suchman (2000) argues with reference to artificial intelligence, the active role of artifacts in the configuration of networks generally seems to imply other human actors just standing offstage. We might also think about more clearly independent agencies at home and how they live with us. Things like animals, plants, and weathers which take us more fully back to the work of the natural scientist. In this arena, Roe (2002), for instance, has used some of these resources to explore the agency of the carrot within domestic food practice. She is concerned with the specific properties that make a carrot fit for human consumption and how our relationships with the peculiar properties and behaviors of the carrot in the home might relate to organic vegetable purchase. Shove (2003) also discusses how the presence of the weather and the seasons can be dealt with at home and at work. In the context of increased air conditioning, what elements of unpredictable weather, she asks, do we want to infiltrate our home spaces? What does the sudden breeze through the window serve to give us, and what, apart from finite energy resources, is lost through the structuring of standardized notions of comfort that deny an encounter with this sort of agency? In my own research (e.g. Hitchings 2002), I am using similar concepts to explore what it is about plants that makes us encourage their liveliness around us at home. I am trying to highlight the ways in which different plants act, and how this is managed symbolically and practically within London. I am interested in the different sorts of entities that have been finding their ways into the domestic garden and what this can tell us about the coordination of home life and the management of nonhuman agency. In the context of a population with more money, but less free time, my aim is to provide an indepth account of how these factors are played out in the relationships and networks surrounding the plants of the garden, when the garden can be both performed as an inert cultural landscape and also a lively set of familiars.

By adopting some elements of this approach, then, another layer of meaning can be revealed where entities can be biological and technical, as well as social, within home relations. They could be, like the tomato, "bio-socio-econonic things" (Harvey *et al.* 2002). They might be symbolic and exchangeable but still maintain a degree of inherent agency that could be allowed more living space within conceptual frameworks that have focused on the social lives of things, or the biography of humanly created commodities (see Appadurai 1988).

This approach is similar to the anthropological stance in its concern for context, but is different in its attention to the agencies inherent within things and our dealings with them according to their specificity. An anthropological approach to the ensemble of entities in the home space can be revealing in its agnosticism, but can also make for difficulties in drawing out such particular agencies. Work developing from this approach focuses on the peculiarity of entities to ask a different set of questions that grapple with this specificity. What is it about the ways in which certain foods behave that might make them appropriate in practice and preparation as edible? What is it about the weather admitted within home lives that we like or dislike? What exactly is it about the way that plants behave that makes us want to tend them? These would be examples of the sort of questions that such a stance can now help us to ask of home activities.

It is also different in its specific alertness to the range of agencies simultaneously at play within individual settings. It is concerned with the fragile networks of association that these agencies are marshaled into to make certain lifestyles and meanings possible and is, therefore, more ready to deal with change within such relationships, rather than assuming a stability of cultural function within a more anthropological lens on home objects. How are our relations with edibility changing? What are the changing infrastructures that allow weather into our homes? How can faster-paced city lives accommodate gradual plant growth?

If Gell, Miller, and anthropologists more generally, see the agency of things to be deeply embedded in their role as social conduits, this alternative stance offers a contextual approach where relations are formed with objects in their own rights and where the ways in which they behave alongside us are foregrounded. The fridge's story was one where the fridge seems reserved and shy as it blends into an infrastructure of provision that quietly evolves as the humans living with them do not quite notice the way in which it ultimately might constrain how they want to live at home. The plant's story is one where more immediately outgoing plants can curry favor with their surrounding humans by showing what attractive displays they might create if given enough care. Of course, this will be different in different contexts and between different particular humans and nonhumans. The point is, however, that attention is now drawn to the ways in which a more inherent agency is received by humans and what this might suggest about our relations with things around us and our willingness to either control them or to let them control us. What is significant is that this stance allows us to productively reveal these developments and to speculate on what this suggests about how humans can come to relate to the nonhuman stranger at home.

CONCLUSION

The materials and matters of the home space can clearly be thought about in many different ways and from many different theoretical vantages. This makes this an exciting area of research and it is through reflecting upon the different ways in which the home may be approached that interesting work can continue being developed. The purpose of this article has been to outline a recent approach to the home that provides a new perspective on matters there. As Knappett (2002) argues, it is not enough to simply state that materials and objects can become alive within social relations. Rather, if this mantra of material culture studies is to be successfully translated into rich empirical work, theorizations of the processes through which they can become evidently alive are necessary. The perspective I have discussed offers one way to do this through an alertness to how and when things can display a more inherent agency within the home.

Derived from science studies, this perspective serves to productively enhance and complement previous work from anthropology on the intimate connections between the people and things that share domestic life. Foregrounding the inherent liveliness of the material world, it draws attention to the ways in which nonhuman agencies and forces will always be close to us, even though, many, including the Bristol homeowners that I started this article with, imaginatively position them as distant. Such an approach, offers a framework of understanding that can help us to empirically traverse the porous membrane between the perceived safe surety of our dwellings, and the unpredictable foreignness of other entities. This stance recasts the domestic as a place where we can certainly make ourselves at home, but where we are always in the presence of an array of intimate nonhuman strangers. Such a project not only allows us to document something of the volatile associations through which home life is organized, but also, in a very real sense, helps develop a social-science narrative that places people more humbly and rightly in a world of relations that we might never fully control.

NOTE

1. Rather than anthropomorphism, where things are thought to be like humans, or technomorphism, where things are thought to be like machines, analytic reconstruction, here, aims to be more circumspect, such that the researcher should always be open to thinking about certain entities in the terms that are most appropriate, rather than the terms to which the researcher is most habituated.

REFERENCES

Akrich, M. 1992. "The De-Scription of Technical Objects." In W. Bijker and J. Law (eds) *Shaping Technology, Building Society: Studies in Sociotechnical Change*, pp. 205–24. Cambridge, MA: MIT Press.

Appadurai, A. (ed.) 1988. *The Social Life of Things: Commodities in Cultural Perspective*. Cambridge: Cambridge University Press.

Bloor, D. 1976. *Knowledge and Social Imaginary*. Chicago, IL: University of Chicago Press.

Buchli, V. 1999. *An Archaeology of Socialism*. Oxford: Berg.

Burgess, J., T. Bedford, K. Hobson, G. Davies and C. M. Harrison. 2003. "(Un)Sustainable Consumption." In F. Berkhout, M. Leach, and

Scoones (eds) *Global Environmental Change and Society*. Cheltenham: Edward Elgar.

Callon, M. 1986. "Some Elements of a Sociology of Translation: Domestication of the Scallops and the Fishermen of Saint Brieuc Bay." In J. Law (ed.) *Power, Action and Belief: A New Sociology of Knowledge?*, pp.196-233. London: Routledge and Kegan Paul.

Clarke, A. 1998. "Window Shopping at Home: Classifieds, Catalogues and New Consumer Skills." In D. Miller (ed.) *Material Cultures: Why Some Things Matter*. Chicago, IL: University of Chicago Press.

Clarke, A. 2001. "The Aesthetics of Social Aspiration." In D. Miller (ed.) *Home Possessions: Material Culture behind Closed Doors*, pp. 23–46. Oxford: Berg.

Collins, H. 1983. "An Empirical Relativist Programme in the Sociology of Scientific Knowledge." In K. Knorr-Cetina and M. Mulkay (eds) *Science Observed: Perspectives on the Social Study of Science*, pp. 85–114. London: Sage.

Cussins, C. 1998. "Ontological Choreography: Agency for Women Patients in an Infertility Clinic." In M. Berg and A. Mol (eds) *Differences in Medicine: Unravelling Practices, Techniques and Bodies*, pp. 166-201. Durham, NC: Duke University Press.

Dant, T. 1999. *Material Culture in the Social World*. Buckingham Open University Press..

Douglas, M. and B. Isherwood. 1979. *The World of Goods: Towards an Anthropology of Consumption*. London: Routledge.

Gell, A. 1998. *Art and Agency: An Anthropological Theory*. Oxford: Caledonian Press.

Hand, M., E. Shove and D. Southerton. 2003. "The Jet Set: Infrastructures, Bodies, Temporal Orders and the Practices of Showering." Paper presented at the British Sociological Association Annual Conference, York University, April 11–13 2003.

Harvey, M., S. Quilley and H. Beynon. 2002. *Exploring the Tomato: Transformations of Nature, Society and Economy*. Cheltenham: Edward Elgar.

Hinchliffe, S. 1997. "Locating Risk: Energy Use, the 'Ideal Home' and the Non-ideal World." *Transactions of the Institute of British Geography* 22(2): 197–209.

Hitchings, R. 2002. "People, Plants, and Performance: On Actor Network Theory and the Material Pleasures of the Private Garden." *Journal of Social and Cultural Geography* 4(1): 99–114.

Iseda, J. 1998. "Scientific Rationality and the 'Even Stronger Programme.'" Paper presented to the International Conference on Science and Technology Studies. Kyoto, Japan.

Jackson, P. 2000. "Rematerializing Social and Cultural Geography." *Journal of Social and Cultural Geography* 1: 9–14.

Knappett, C. 2002. "Photographs, Skeuomorphs and Marionettes: Some Thoughts on Mind, Agency and Object." *Journal of Material Culture* 7(1): 97–117.

Knorr-Cetina, K. 1981. *The Manufacture of Knowledge: An Essay on the Constructed and Contextual Nature of Science*. Oxford: Pergamon.

Latour, B. 1988. *The Pasteurisation of France*. Cambridge, MA: Harvard University Press.

Latour, B. 1992. "One More Turn After the Social Turn: Easing Science Studies into the Non-modern World." In E. McMullin (ed.) *Social Dimensions of Science*, pp. 272–92. Paris: Notre Dame.

Latour, B. 1993. *We Have Never Been Modern*. New York: Harvester: Wheatsheaf.

Latour, B. 1997. *Aramis, ou l'Amour des Techniques*. Paris: Éditions de la Découverte.

Latour, B. 2000. "When Things Strike Back: A Possible Contribution of 'Science Studies' to the Social Sciences." *British Journal of Sociology* 51(1): 107–23.

Laurier, E. and C. Philo. (1998). *Meet You at Junction 17: A Socio-technical and Spatial Study of the Mobile Office*. Glasgow: Department of Geography, University of Glasgow and Swindon: ESRC.

Laurier, E. and C. Philo. 1999. "X-morphising: A Review Essay of Bruno Latour's 'Aramis or the Love of Technology'." *Environment and Planning A* 31: 1047–71.

Law, J. 1994. *Organising Modernity*. Oxford: Blackwell.

Law, J. and V. Singleton. 2000. "This is Not an Object." Centre for Science Studies, Lancaster University. http://www.comp.lancs.ac.uk/sociology/soc032jl.html.

Lynch, M. 1991. "Method: Measurement—Ordinary and Scientific Measurement as Ethnomethodological Phenomena." In G. Button (ed.) *Ethnomethodology and the Human Sciences*. Cambridge: Cambridge University Press.

Lynch, M. 1993. *Scientific Practice and Ordinary Action: Ethnomethodology and Social Studies of Science*. Cambridge: Cambridge University Press.

Miller, D. 1995. "Consumption and commodities." *Annual Review of Anthropology* 24: 141–61.

Miller, D. 1998a. *A Theory of Shopping*. Oxford: Polity Press.

Miller, D. 1998. "Why Some Things Matter." In D. Miller (ed.) *Material Cultures: Why Some Things Matter*, pp. 3–21. Chicago, IL: University of Chicago Press. .

Miller, D. 2001a. "Behind Closed Doors." In D. Miller (ed.) *Home Possessions: Material Culture and the Home*, pp. 1–22. Oxford: Berg.

Miller, D. 2001b. "Possessions." In D. Miller (ed.) *Home Possessions: Material Culture and the Home*, pp. 107–22. Oxford: Berg.

Roe, E. 2003. "Things Become Food: Practices of Organic Food Consumers." Unpublished PhD Thesis, University of Bristol.

Shapin, S and S. Shaffer. 1989. *Leviathan and the Air Pump: Hobbes, Boyle and the Experimental Life*. Princeton, NJ: Princeton University Press.

Shove, E. 1999. "Notes on Comfort, Cleanliness and Convenience." Paper presented at the ESF summer school on Consumption Everyday Life and Sustainability. www.lancs.acluk/users/scistud/esf/sve.html.

Shove, E. 2003. "Resources and Services: Consuming Energy in the Built Environment." Paper presentation to Technonatures Symposium Department of Sociology, Goldsmiths College. June 26 2003.

Shove, E. and D. Southerton. 2000. "Defrosting the Freezer—From Novelty to Convenience—A Narrative of Normalisation." *Journal of Material Culture* 53: 301–19.

Suchman, L. 2000. "Human/Machine Reconsidered." Department of Sociology, Lancaster University. http://www.comp.lancs.ac.uk/sociology/soc040ls.html.

Tilley, C., S. Hamilton, S. Harrison and E. Anderson. 2000. "Nature, Culture, Clitter: Distinguishing between Cultural and Geomorphological Landscapes; The Case of Hilltop Tors in South-west England." *Journal of Material Culture* 5(2): 197–224.

Whatmore, S. 2002. *Hybrid Geographies: Natures, Cultures, Spaces.* London: Routledge.

Williams, R. 1973. *The Country and the City.* Oxford: Oxford University Press.

Woolgar, S. 1988. *Science: The Very Idea.* London: Routledge.

Zukin, S. 1991. *Landscapes of Power: From Detroit to Disneyworld.* Berkeley, OA: University of California Press.

HOME CULTURES   VOLUME 1, ISSUE 2.
PP 187–208

SUZANNE REIMER AND DEBORAH LESLIE

IDENTITY, CONSUMPTION, AND THE HOME

SUZANNE REIMER IS A
LECTURER IN GEOGRAPHY AT
THE UNIVERSITY OF HULL.
CURRENT RESEARCH
INTERESTS INCLUDE THE
CRITICAL EVALUATION OF THE
ROLE OF "CULTURAL
PRODUCTS" INDUSTRIES IN
LOCAL AND REGIONAL
ECONOMIC DEVELOPMENT;
ETHICAL ISSUES IN
CONSUMPTION; AND
KNOWLEDGE FLOWS AMONG
ACTORS ACROSS THE
COMMODITY NETWORK.

DEBORAH LESLIE IS ASSOCIATE
PROFESSOR IN THE
DEPARTMENT OF GEOGRAPHY,
UNIVERSITY OF TORONTO. SHE
IS PRESENTLY UNDERTAKING A
STUDY OF GEOGRAPHIES OF
DESIGN AND NETWORKS OF
CREATIVITY IN CANADIAN
CITIES.

Despite a rich literature on the power
dynamics of households within domestic
space, the specificities of home
consumption have been undertheorized
within broader accounts of consumption
and identity. Consumption frequently is
conceptualized as a individualistic
process, undertaken by a single self-
reflexive actor. Focusing upon the
purchasing, acquisition and display of
furniture and other domestic goods, this
article reflects upon the role of home
consumption in identity construction
within both individual households as well
as different household groups. We argue
that home consumption at times may be
equally important to both individual and
multiple households—despite
conventional associations between
homemaking and the nuclear family.
Notions of the self may be dissipated in

collective provisioning by households consisting of couples, although fractures and conflict also may undermine general agreements about shared space. Both the making of the landscape inside the home and the narration of this making are ongoing projects undertaken within and through the diverse webs of relationship among individuals within a household.

INTRODUCTION

The central focus of this article is upon the articulation of identity through home consumption. Our main concern is to utilize the specific example of the purchase for and use of goods in the home in order to interrogate different understandings of the relationship between consumption and identity. Many contemporary sociological accounts have focused upon the creation of *self*-identity through consumption. Particularly in work which has foregrounded a late-twentieth-century displacement of identity formation from the sphere of production to that of consumption (Bauman 1998; Giddens 1991; Lash and Friedman 1996), emphasis is placed upon the ways in which men and women construct identities through individual consumption practices and habits. However, there also has been some suggestion that identity construction through consumption may not be entirely individualistic and self-directed: Carrier (1995: 15, emphasis added), for example, notes that ". . . where people shop and the ways they shop can be important for changing . . . things from impersonal commodities to possessions that embody the shopper's identity and location *in a web of personal relationships.*" Consumption therefore, is shaped at least in part through relationships with others. Our article's focus on home consumption provides a counter to portrayals which tend to overemphasize individual lifestyle or identity "choice" and offers the potential to shed light on the diverse ways in which consuming identities are constructed.

Through the article we conceptualize home consumption as the purchasing, acquisition, and display of furniture and other domestic goods.[1] We follow relatively recent understandings of consumption as "a social process whereby people relate to goods and artefacts in complex ways, transforming their meaning as they incorporate them in their lives through successive cycles of use and reuse" (Jackson and Holbrook 1995: 1914; see also Pred 1996). "Home consumption" therefore extends beyond simply initial decisions about new furniture acquisition: we use the term to encompass the range of ways in which women and men obtain and use furnishings in the home. In contrast to clothes and food, which articulate closely with an individual body, furniture and furnishings are distinctive in that their acquisition culminates in the production of the domestic interior. Thus, home consumption is particularly interesting because of its specific context: domestic space.

Across a range of disciplines—including anthropology, sociology, geography, social history, and design history—many writers increasingly have emphasized the complex entanglements of domesticity within Western households (Chapman and Hockey, 1999; Cieraad, 1999; Dowling and Pratt 1993; Madigan and Munro 1996; Putnam and Newton 1990). Yet despite a rich literature on the power dynamics of households within domestic space, the specificities of *home* consumption have been undertheorized within broader accounts of consumption and identity. Consumption frequently continues to be conceptualized as an individualistic process, undertaken by a single, self-reflexive actor (see also Gronow and Warde 2001: 2; Shove and Warde 2002: 234–5).

Our central intent in this article is to contribute to understandings of the complex dynamics of consumption practices within the home. As Valentine (1999: 492) has argued in relation to research on domestic food consumption, "[the home] is a site of individual, but also collective (household or 'family') consumption, where the goods purchased and the meanings and uses ascribed to them are negotiated, and sometimes contested, between household members." In summarizing contributions to an edited collection on the material culture of the home, Miller (2001: 4) similarly reflects: "the private [is] more a turbulent sea of constant negotiation rather than simply some haven for the self." Below, we illuminate the complexities of home consumption within domestic spaces which may be shared, negotiated and contested. We consider the extent to which notions of the self might be dissipated when family members engage in collective provisioning, and reflect upon negotiated arrangements amongst households which may not always be made up of heterosexual couples or nuclear families.

Throughout, we seek to emphasize the "work" of consumption involved in the ongoing creation and re-creation of identity (Miller 1991). Additionally, as Miller (1998: 146–7) has argued, the inalienability of commodities results from the object becoming part of personification through the act of consumption:

> if persons and relationships become the primary medium through which we achieve a sense of the transcendent or the inalienable, then in turn any objects which express persons or relationships become the vehicle for expressing these higher values. Ironically then, it is the alienable commodity that in our society becomes the mode of realizing, through a process of subjectification, our imagination of the inalienable.

This allows Miller to stress that specific goods need not directly "symbolize persons or identity. Shopping is an active praxis which intervenes and constitutes as well as referring back to relationships" (1998: 147). Home consumption practices thus may not be simply reflective of an individual consuming self, but also have the potential to mold relationships between individuals in the home.

The article draws upon material from a project examining the dynamics of the home furnishings commodity chain in the United Kingdom and Canada. The work was influenced by arguments about connections between sites through which commodities move: as Fine and Leopold (1993: 15) have indicated, "commodities are socially constructed not only in their meaning but also in the material practices by which they are produced, distributed and ultimately consumed." The empirical study conducted between 1997 and 2001 included interviews with furniture manufacturers, retailers, designers, magazine editors, and consumers, although in this article we focus upon discussions with consumers. Consumer interviewees were obtained primarily via networks which originated from retailers, including a snowball sampling technique and personal contacts. A specific interest in retailers and manufacturers which emphasized innovative styling, materials, and production techniques led us to pursue consumers who had dealings with "design-led" retailers. At least in part as a result, interviewees were predominantly middle-class to upper middle-class urban dwellers.[2] Further, although we originally had anticipated that national variation in home consumption practices might be of greater import, we ultimately could discern no noticeable differences in the ways in which Canadian and British interviewees reflected upon the relationship between home consumption and identity construction.[3] Interviews were open-ended, unstructured, and highly conversational; and discussions also involved informal tours of the home.

We begin by considering theoretical tensions within prevalent accounts of consumption and identity at a general level, before turning to reflect upon the specific case of the home and home consumption. The remainder of the article underscores the making of homes both by individuals as well as by couples; the ways that a range of household groups interact through material objects in the home; and the ways in which the formation and dissolution of households shape the nature of consumption practices in the home. Following Miller *et al.* (1998: 24), we emphasize how individuals "narrate their identities" through home consumption, "rather than simply inferring [their] identities from the purchases they make." This is a particularly important strategy given the historic importance of discourses surrounding home*making*. That is, the project of constructing identity in and through the home is an ongoing process, in which individuals and households "*actively try out different sides of the self*" (Löfgren 1990: 32, emphasis added).

CONSUMPTION AND IDENTITY

Much contemporary discussion of identity formation in late modernity has taken cues from authors such as Giddens (1991, 1992) and Beck (1992), who have foregrounded the reflexive making of the self. Although not specifically directed towards the relationship between consumption and identity, the implication of such work is that the construction of the self depends at least in part upon the choices that we make as consumers (Slater 1997: 91). As Slater argues, a reflexive project "involves unremitting self-monitoring, self-scrutiny, planning and ordering of all elements of our lives, appearances and performances in order to marshal them into a coherent narrative." Thus, not only are we required to choose between different types of selves, but also the "post-traditional world" requires that we "constitute ourselves as a self who chooses, a consumer" (Slater 1997: 91). In a detraditionalized and individualized world, individuals expect (and are expected to) focus much more specifically upon their own project of self-identity.

For some authors, this direction of attention towards the individual self is said to imply a significant reworking of relationships and indeed of love itself (Beck and Beck-Gernsheim 1995; Giddens, 1992). Giddens (1992: 58), for example, suggests that in contrast to older variants of romantic love, a "pure relationship" now involves

> a situation where a social relation is entered into for its own sake, for what can be derived by each person from a sustained association with another; and which is continued only in so far as it is thought by both parties to deliver enough satisfaction for each individual to stay within it.

Yet as Miller (1998) has suggested, Giddens' (1992) portrayal of individualized, self-directed practice (which may include the practice of consumption) in fact sits uneasily with the argument that relationships between couples increasingly involve negotiation and explicit dialogue. Miller questions how two apparently "self-directed" partners can "participate in a relationship which may demand not only considerable compromise but also the subsumption and to a degree the elimination of that same individuality" (1998: 119).

Miller's (1998: 123) own resolution of this contradiction is to indicate that in routine shopping for clothing and household goods (predominantly conducted by women), individuality tends to be sacrificed for devotion to another. Shopping is not an individualistic or individualizing act, tied to the subjectivity of the shopper. Rather it

> is dominated by your imagination of others, of what they desire of you and their response to you; it is about relationship to those who require something of you. Often these are relationships of devotion, mainly routine devotion, that may be deep or may be superficial, and are mainly taken for granted . . . (Miller 1998: 3–4).

Consumers do not merely buy goods for others, but aim to influence others to become the kind of person who desires the items being purchased: "buying goods is often as much about others in the family as it is about the shopper, especially for women" (Miller et al. 1998: 17). This suggests to Miller (1998: 122–3) that in contrast to Giddens'

(1992) emphasis on a more "democratic" confluent love, shopping in north London, at least (see also Clarke 2001) reveals the dominance of agapic love, or the loss of self through merging with a beloved other.

Rather than pursue further Miller's (1998) account of the direct role of love and relationships within domestic consumption practices, we wish instead to foreground a remaining theoretical tangle within existing discussions of consumption and identity formation: the tension—and indeed slippage—between considerations of the formation of (individual) self-identity and the shaping of (collective) household identity. Bourdieu's (1984) work, for example, is derived from responses by individuals, although it is sometimes invoked in discussions which seek to investigate patterns of household consumption more broadly. Studies such as Lunt and Livingstone's also amalgamate analyses of "the meanings of personal *and* domestic objects" (1992: 64, emphasis added). While Löfgren argues that "homemaking has become very closely related to identity formation," he is also concerned to situate homemaking within the emergence of a *"family* project," in which "the family is constantly being repaired and renovated" (1990: 32).

There remains a question as to how we might understand and represent the diversity of engagement with home consumption practices, both within and among households. Are there potential tensions between individually directed and "family"-oriented home consumption? Further, if consuming goods for the home is always seen to be tied to the idea of producing and sustaining the family, how might we conceptualize the "consuming interests" of single-person households? For Miller (1998: 121), provisioning by single women is not viewed as individualistic, but rather single women are seen to be consuming "almost always with an eye to the imagination and the potential of another." Their "shopping is directed to the household itself that simply happens, for the moment, to have only one person in it" (1998: 121)

Although we are drawn to some elements of Miller's (1998) emphasis on the construction of relationships through consumption and shopping practices, we have some concerns about his representation of provisioning by single women, which appears to represent an overly conservative view of household formation. Similarly, whilst Johnson (1996: 461) emphasizes married Australian women's "active practising of place" through the construction of the domestic environment, we would like to recuperate aspirations for "a home of one's own" from traditional associations of homemaking with the heterosexual nuclear family. Below, we consider the consuming identities of a range of different types of household.

HOME CONSUMPTION: THE HOME AND IDENTITY

Furniture and household goods are centrally involved in the construction of something called "home" (Cieraad 1999; Miller 2001). Rather than simply a commodity consumed within the home, furniture is the home. Seeley *et al.*, for example, have argued that furniture should be seen as the most important element in individual understandings of home: "it is really the moveables which create the air of homeliness, and which are psychologically immoveable, rather than the physically rooted house" (1956: 58). A furniture designer interviewed for our research similarly noted that

> people seem to be a little bit more complacent I think about architecture . . . they have their apartment and it might not be the one they really want, or they have their house and it might not be the one they really want, but they can kind of realize what they want through the furniture . . . you can also change it . . . more easily. It's much more personal . . .You can take the furniture you have and make a new setting . . . I think we tend to build a profile of ourselves through the furniture that we buy.

There are multiple connections between consuming bodies in the space of the home. Furniture consumption frequently is negotiated between individuals and can come to embody shared and negotiated identity. Furniture is tactile as well as visual, and items such as sofas and beds may be explicitly tied to notions of shared intimacy in the home. This means that disentangling—or at least recognizing a multiplicity of— subjectivities in the home is a difficult task. As de Grazia (1996: 8–9) notes, the subject has not attracted a good deal of attention:

> . . . [the] process of negotiation among persons with an affective as well as a material stake in this joint enterprise—usually wife and husband, but also older and younger generations—is as yet little explored, though it would seem to shape profoundly what kinds of goods are purchased, what services are delegated to or re-appropriated from the market, and what values are attached to goods in the pursuit of family well-being.

Within Western households consisting of couples, the notion of home as a shared project leading to the construction of a shared identity has carried a strong weight. In the UK in the 1950s, DIY became an essential part of homemaking: young couples forming households in the immediate aftermath of the Second World War sought expression through home decoration and design. Manufacturers often exploited the notion of DIY as a collective project in their advertising. Dulux, for example, shifted away from the promotion of the product—a tin of paint which had the weight of the manufacturer's expertise behind it—to portraying young couples painting together (BBC2 1997; see also MacDonald and Porter 1990). Through the latter part of the twentieth century, the purchase of furniture was seen to be the responsibility of a female consumer, and the notion of homemaking remained highly gendered (Madigan *et al*. 1990), but the final outcome of home consumption was meant to represent a collective identity. These idealized notions about negotiated decision-making amongst heterosexual partners and about the creation of "shared" space have been remarkably persistent within Western cultures, leading to pressures on households to portray homemaking as a joint undertaking. In practice, however, the idea of "negotiation" "may create a misleading impression, as [. . .] differing rationales may be accommodated in a shared result" (Putnam 1999: 148). What may be represented as a collective consuming identity may in fact be the outcome of changing divisions of homemaking labor and/or shifting individual investments in home consumption.[4]

Heterogeneous engagements with home consumption in the twenty-first century undoubtedly have been shaped by changing patterns of household formation (and dissolution). Much previous work on the home and domestic space broadly has taken heterosexual, nuclear family households as its focus (see, for example, Madigan and Munro 1996; Munro and Madigan 1999; Parr 1999b; Pratt 1981; Shove 1999). Although heterosexual couples formed the largest subgroup, the marital status and sexuality of our interviewees was not entirely uniform. Further, interviewees often had engaged in a series of homemaking exercises, as personal circumstances changed. In order to unravel stories of home consumption, we begin by considering the extent to which our interviewees viewed the home as reflective of individual identity. We then consider respondents' constructions of collective identity within shared domestic spaces. Transitions in household formation—and concomitant transformations in home consumption activities—are addressed in the final section of the article.

INDIVIDUAL IDENTITY AND THE HOME

Our interviewees' narratives begin with the example of a single woman, Chloe, who is in her mid-twenties and works as a retail manager.[5] At the time we spoke to her, Chloe lived in a two-bedroom rented shared flat and was preparing to move to a rented shared house. This move would involve a number of pieces of furniture and accessories—Chloe was particularly enthusiastic about design and style in the home. She typically obtained furniture by having it made for her by her father but frequently researched the furniture market for ideas to be copied, using shops and magazines as browsing spaces to develop a knowledge of styles. She also drew upon knowledge of contemporary design acquired through a general interest in art and design and an educational background in practical art and design history. In purchasing and acquiring goods for the home, Chloe combined a relatively minimal style with simple individual pieces. Her look involved a mix of contemporary and retro styles, with accessories from the 1950s, 1960s and 1970s chosen for a more "classic" and "timeless" feel rather than as distinctively "period" pieces. Through changes in residence, and despite sharing a home with one or more other people, Chloe emphasized the development of a distinctive individual style through home consumption. Contrary to Miller's (1998) claim that single women's provisioning represents a way to refuse rather than maintain individualism, Chloe did not view her experiences and practices as purely transitory or temporary, nor influenced by the desire for a partner.

Sarah, a single mid-forties charity organization worker, described her two-bedroom inner-city early Edwardian terrace as having a "vaguely cottage feel." In both this and previous houses she had sought to "decorate to its age," although a number of elements—including a turquoise and gold cabinet hiding the television and stereo and a collection of 1950s plastic radios—contributed to an eclectic, rather than a definitively period style. Sarah emphasized the importance of defining (individual) identity at home in response to uniform and bureaucratic styling at work:

> I think perhaps particularly now also because you . . . workplaces are becoming more and more the same; you walk into any office building now and they've all got fake maple desks or Formica top type of desks, they're all sitting in the same chairs. And it's . . . the days of finding bits of furniture like that [pointing to a roll-top chest] in offices is . . . just wouldn't happen. And with things like hot-desking where you don't even have a desk to call your own, I suppose having an identity in your own home becomes all that much more important because you're running out of places that you can use to extend your identity. I think it's really important for people to be able to make that statement. This is me.

In furnishing and maintaining her home, Sarah's attention was not directed towards the imagination of another—a greater influence appeared to be changes and disruptions at work. Having had to move jobs several times following a period of local government restructuring, Sarah's current homemaking activities appeared more closely bound up with the creation of a stable, calm non-work environment. Her prized roll-top desk in fact had been salvaged from a prior local authority employer following an office reshuffle. Here, the creation and narration of individual identity in the home was in part inflected by activities and pursuits outside the domestic sphere.[6]

Even when their homes were furnished with pieces handed down from other family members, interviewees often stressed that the overall "feeling" of the home strongly reflected their individual identity. Mario, a single, forty-something male living in a late-Victorian house, emphasized in response to a question about inherited furniture: "no it's not [my parents' and grandparents'] identity. No I think it really is mine. It's my stamp of who I am by looking around." Like Sarah, Mario also was enthusiastic about purchasing period antiques, again because they were seen to "go with the character of the house, the neighbourhood." For certain households, at certain moments, individual identity construction may reach beyond the immediate confines of the home, with decisions about interior and exterior (including the local neighborhood) intricately entwined.

Thirty-something Barbara lived in a developer-converted city center "loft" apartment and also had decorated her home with a variety of gifts and acquisitions from other family members and friends. Keen on scanning home interiors magazines, Barbara was enthusiastic about colorful, modern pieces as well as a table inherited from an aunt who had died. The table originally formed part of a set that Barbara described as "almost look[ing] like a Japanese or a Chinese type of table look which is really in style now too." She was "destroyed" that she had given away the other two tables prior to her move to the loft. Barbara noted that although her mother occasionally purchased small items of furniture for her,

> I come in here and it's just me for sure. And I think when my mum buys things for me, she knows my taste. Like she would buy those [a different group of] tables, she would buy them for herself. She knows my taste.

The activity and creativity which is seen to be a part of homemaking is such that even if goods have a provenance which is not necessarily a direct purchase by the owner, individuals see their own style reflected in objects.

Recent changes in the nature of furniture retailing away from the matched three-piece suite towards a more eclectic (albeit carefully styled) format often have presented consumers with distinctive "lifestyle" settings (Leslie and Reimer 2003a, b). Paul, who lived in a shared rented flat with an artist and a financial investor, was particularly scathing about the extent to which the Canadian mass-market furnishing/clothing/homeware retailer Caban (Figure 1; see also www.caban.com) sought to market a uniform, prepackaged lifestyle to consumers. Although both he and his male flatmates had purchased pieces from both Caban and Ikea for reasons of economy, he preferred buying what he described as "vintage" furniture from second-hand shops:

> people that aren't artists [. . .] maybe they'd want something that, maybe they're not conscious of trends and how people are buying stuff from Ikea everyday and buying stuff from Caban and now that's popular with people. Everyone's doing it, right? But I'm way too conscious of that I guess just being an artist like I think about that all the time and I hate it. Like don't want to have anything to do with Ikea or Caban even though I bought this stuff.

With a relatively new career in an animation studio following art college, Paul's living arrangements predominantly reflected financial

circumstances as well as age. At a particular stage of life, it was important for Paul to reiterate a sharply distinctive (artistic) individuality in
part through a refusal to identify with mass-produced furniture. He
emphasized the importance of creating an individual style in the home—
even as he "admitted" to purchasing items from mass-market retailers.

Figure 1
Caban (Granville Street,
Vancouver, Canada). *Source:*
Suzanne Reimer.

SHARED SPACE

Narrating Shared Identities

Furniture has the potential to become a shared commodity within
multiple-person households, arguably rendering questions of identity
construction more complex than for other, more individualized, types
of goods such as clothing or cars. We now turn specifically to focus upon
joint provisioning strategies. Households consisting of couples often
constructed apparently uniform narratives about the selection of goods.
Married couple Gary and Jo could not even imagine a situation where
they did not agree:

> Gary: I mean I can't honestly remember us ever when we first
> got married, me saying I like it this way, and you had better like
> it like that mate . . .
>
> Jo: there is no competition
>
> Gary: or you are not marrying me . . .

For women and men who present themselves as relatively egalitarian couples, it becomes important to emphasize a commonality of taste which in turn becomes a significant expression of their existence as a compatible couple in love (Miller 1998: 27). Thus it is sometimes difficult to unpack potential differentiations between individually directed and family-oriented home consumption:

> we both tend to like the same things so I suppose we are lucky that way. [. . .] rather than [. . .] one of us being minimalist and the other being a Laura Ashley freak . . . But I suppose when you first look at the house this is a house that is a combination of two people's ideas . . . (Jill, married)

Fifty-something Carol and Andrew lived in a medium-sized detached house in a suburban neighborhood. Within the last five years, they had switched the location of the kitchen and dining room as well as extensively remodeling the master bedroom and ensuite bathroom. Their furnishing style falls somewhere between the "contemporary" and the "traditional"—they are aware of current trends but are most concerned about comfort and "fit" of their furniture. Our discussions during the interview primarily revolved around the couple's shared furniture, rather than any furniture purchased during each of their previous marriages. Emphasis frequently was placed on the egalitarian processes of shopping for furniture:

> Carol: we do it together. Yes.
>
> Andrew: yeah, we do. That might be unusual, I don't know.
>
> Carol: I don't know . . . I guess Tim and Sue, our friends, they do stuff together too, although Tim will defer to Sue because he thinks she has more decorating style than he does. I don't know about that . . . but . . . we do go together. Sometimes we'll end up with Andrew's choice, sometimes we'll end up with my choice. Most cases . . . I don't recall a time when we couldn't compromise, one way or the other. That one was so strong that it had to be this. I don't think that happens very often.

Carol and Andrew strive to narrate home consumption as a truly shared practice, in which individual self-identities are subsumed within a representation of collective experience.

For fifty-something office worker Lucy, joint decision-making was emphasized within the discussion of a previous relationship. At the time of interview, Lucy lived in a two-bedroom flat in an outer-city neighborhood, having moved several times following her separation from her husband Mark.

> When we first got married [in the 1970s] there was a lot of that blonde furniture around. And we really didn't like it and then

we found the Vilas maple and it was warm, it was a warm colour.[7] [. . .] And yeah it was fun, so we did buy it together. We both liked it. We would always go shopping [together] except for my twenty-fourth birthday, Mark bought a piece, a chest on chest for the bedroom and there was a present in every drawer (laughter). So you see there were good times! Twenty-four red roses and then a present in every drawer (laughter). Eight drawers or something . . . Because it was something that we'd wanted, this chest on chest, we'd looked at it and as I say we had the catalogue and we'd always be looking over the catalogue, oh what should we get next and you know look at this and isn't that nice and we'd have the approximate value and the price, the retail price for it, so then he surprised me with that.

Within the same story not only do we hear about shared tastes in color and style, and about the enjoyment of choosing furniture together, but also we are told about a particular chest of drawers which became a surprise birthday gift. Even as an individual gift, however, the chest is represented as something "we'd wanted." The importance of compatible homemaking through joint purchase is stressed, albeit within the context of a relationship which had broken down.

Susan, a married insurance clerk in her late thirties, recounted a tale which shifted between individual choice and notions of "compromise:"

I've probably got the ultimate say at the very end (laughing), but we both look. My husband, he likes to shop too. He goes through all the shops and at the end of the day when it came to the final decision of, well we each got a chair, so he got to pick what kind of a chair he wanted and I got the over-stuffed chair. [. . .] But we both . . .I think in the long run I got the final say, but he was in the decision process (laughter). Because I would have pouted if I didn't get it! Cause he's not happy with the couches. I mean because we just downsized and we're in a smaller house. We bought the couch just after we moved and he swore it was too big and probably is, but I don't care, I like it, it stays.

Thus the articulation of compromise does occasionally stray from a more positively inflected situation of negotiated decision-making to the narration of a process which is somewhat more conflictual. Another married interviewee commented that: "You know for good or bad . . . if you are living with somebody else in the same house, you can't do what you both want and sometimes you have to compromise. You might not go for the first thing you thought of. You might go for the sixth thing you thought of because your partner prefers to look at that." Susan, quoted above, noted that her husband could "pick what kind of electronic stuff that goes in the house, because I don't really care; as long as I know how to turn it on, it's OK." This suggests that although couples might come to general agreement about shared space, self-identities are not entirely suppressed in collective home provisioning. That is, despite cultural pressures to "subsume differences in a joint life project" (Putnam 1999: 148), there may be moments when one household member might relinquish their own preferences to another's tastes. We now want to foreground ambiguities and inconsistencies contained within the household as a "consuming unit" by examining a number of cases of conflict and tension.

Fractures, Conflict, and Tension

Fractures in collective identity are particularly visible in interviewees' discussions when narratives drift between choices made by "I" and "we:"

> [. . .] in general *we* buy what we like, so *we* see something, for instance these chairs here (Florence Knoll upholstered) [. . .] And *I* was in Martin's store one day and *I* saw that chair and *I* loved it—like you know *I* said *I'll* have that chair (emphasis added).

Jack and Sue lived in a suburban bungalow which they had extensively refurbished in a distinctly international modern style. Through the interview, Jack made numerous references to the influences of Sue's academic background in art history and design—as well as her Italian family "heritage"—on their joint furniture purchases and general style in the home. Although their shopping often was done together, it is notable that in the above example, Jack appeared to have made the decision on his own.

Sarah, the charity worker described previously, was explicitly reflective about the complexities of joint decision-making:

> I think when you're living with somebody, there is this sort of negotiation and compromise that goes on, and I think it's quite important that you can agree. 'Cause I have had friends who haven't been able to . . . sort of very, very different tastes, and they've ended up going down the route, right you can do that room and I will do that room (laughing). So that they both feel that they've had a chance to have their tastes expressed. But there's always a lot of slagging off that goes on! Oh, YOU chose that, didn't you . . . that kind of thing. Which I suppose must be . . . not having been a situation of violently disagreeing with somebody, you know I've never had to live with something that I object to. But . . . I can see that it could be quite annoying. It must be very difficult in something like a living room. Where you both spend a great deal of time, coming to an agreement on what that's going to look like if you've both got different tastes, must be a nightmare. Either that or you end up with a space that nobody's happy with.

Here Sarah reads others' experiences as being markedly different from her own. Conflict between members of a compatible couple was not something with which she felt familiar. Although recently separated from a female partner, they had together enjoyed spending considerable time refurbishing a five-bedroom early-Victorian townhouse in period style. Fractures in her own story emerged later on in the conversation, when Sarah indicated that she "quite enjoyed taking a break from the relentless, we need something to go in that corner; really need something to match *that*." In her new house she took pleasure from having a distinct space of her own, decorating eclectically, and collecting pieces of furniture which were particularly important to her.

The home is not, of course, a singular uniform space, and interviewees often sought to claim different rooms or areas of the home as their "own." Recognizing such micro-geographies of domestic consumption is important, for as Shove (1999: 131) argues, "for the most part, analyses of housing routinely stop at the front door" and assume a coherent "household unit." Munro and Madigan (1999: 116) suggest that in practice there is often a sharp conflict between "the assumption of a shared, democratic family life [. . .] implicit in the physical design of houses, and the aspirations of those who have chosen to live in them." In the married household of Brian and Sophie, Brian noted that "the bedroom it's sort of her territory . . . I'm not allowed to keep any of my own stuff in the bedroom. If piles of books sit there too long, I find them in the hall eventually and that's just because the room is very small and I do have another part of the house where I can keep my own junk." Although Brian suggests that he finds the demarcation of space restrictive, it also is important to note that it is most often women who lack space of their own in the home. Madigan *et al.* (1990: 631–2) stress, for example, that while children in more affluent homes increasingly have individual rooms, "adults continue to share bedrooms and public space." They argue that "in one sense a woman controls the whole house; but in another she may feel she owns nothing personally but her side of the wardrobe" (Whitehorn 1987, cited in Madigan *et al.* 1990: 632). Many of the women Munro and Madigan (1999) interviewed also were required to suppress their own need for privacy in the face of pressures to maintain conventional values of the home as communal family "haven" (see also Hunt 1995).

Rather than home always being a uniform, shared project (Löfgren 1990), it can also be a site of contestation, even for couples who emphasize the shared project of homemaking, or stress that compromise between two people is necessary. Dave and Fiona lived in the top-floor flat of a vast detached house in an expensive residential neighborhood. They shared an interest in modern design and throughout most of the interview narrated their home furnishings style as an entirely collective project. Yet at one point during the discussion, when Dave was describing the sleek lines of their dining table with its intricate system of drop leaves, Fiona whispered into the tape recorder to indicate that she was mystified by his obsession with the object—"it looks like my gran's!"

It is important to reiterate that shared households do not always and everywhere and at all stages of the life course consist of heterosexual couples. Thirty-something Dan, for example, highlighted conflicts over the type and arrangement of home possessions in a number of shared houses in which he had lived previously. In the first: "I think the one concession was that Patricia had a huge television. It was massive— like about 28 inches and she plonked that right in the middle of the room and I hate having televisions as the focus and I hate big tellies— that was horrid but is was a concession." Unequal power relations between individuals potentially can contribute to household conflict in such situations: in a second house, Dan noted that:

> the two women I moved in with they sort of had enough furni-
> ture for a room but I had lots of old bits of furniture people had
> given me and stuff so we moved in and it was unfurnished and
> I sort of said well can I put this here, can I put that there and
> everything was agreed democratically but then after a couple
> of weeks we had a huge row and I was accused of taking over:
> "it's your house; we don't feel we are part of it." Because it was
> completely my style, [. . .] they said I could do it . . . and then
> they just sort of hated it.

Inhabiting or occupying another person's furniture may be profoundly disorientating for those who have not had a say in the creation of space. Although Dan and his housemates had attempted to pursue a democratic decision-making process in furnishing collective living spaces, individual preferences ultimately dominated.

CHANGING ROOMS/CHANGING SPACES

In the final section of this article we consider how changes in living arrangements may rupture and transform the connections between identity and the home. Several stories of changed household circumstances have emerged in the discussions above, but we would now like to focus specifically on the ways in which people explained specific transformations in home consumption. Thirty-something David lived with a lodger in a terraced inner-city house which made strong use of very bold colors in both paint and furnishings. At the time of interview he worked for a children's charity, although he had studied architecture at university and continued to be an avid reader of design and architecture magazines. In another house, in a "previous life," David and his partner had been living with assorted chairs and a single futon:

> . . . but my partner at the time just kept moaning about the fact
> that every sort of chair is not very good for being like a sofa
> [. . .] so then I went out and said right, blow the credit cards

> and I am going to get this [. . .] and I got it ordered and thought
> brilliant and then sort of arranged for it to be delivered just after
> Christmas and then Simon split with me, . . . I got the sofa and
> no person to go on it so that was ridiculous, but it was done.

Particularly when purchased together, furniture often becomes intimately associated with a relationship. Although David enthusiastically had pursued the creation of a distinctive individual style on his own in his new home, he continued to view the relatively expensive sofa as a redundant purchase, which appeared to make the loss of his partner seem more acute.

A change in a relationship very often results in the reconstruction of home; destabilizing the collective "project" and sometimes necessitating a new round of consumption and/or changes in taste and style. Lucy, whose enthusiasm for maple furniture we have already encountered, had furnished the flat in which she now lived on her own with new furniture of relatively traditional styling. Items included striped green and cream sofas from a national department store, and a small round dining table and chairs of light wood with woven fabric seats. Her bedroom furniture consisted of a box spring divan and white fiberboard chests of drawers. In part because the flat had considerable built-in cupboard space in the front entrance hall and each of the two bedrooms, Lucy felt little need to purchase additional pieces of furniture. More importantly, perhaps, she had left all of the furniture from her previous relationship with her ex-husband and professed no longer to be concerned about issues of home decoration and style: "you can't get me out of a bicycle store, or an outdoor store, but furniture stores I have no desire to go in them." At the same time, she did reflect that she might have put more thought into the purchase of a small dining table:

> afterwards, I realised that I should have bought something with
> a leaf in it, but I didn't, because I could not, at that point in my
> life understand why I would ever want a large table again! (laugh-
> ter) . . . Two people max. So that was a mistake, but you know,
> that was the time . . . the period I was in.

Attitudes towards home consumption inevitably will undergo potentially quite complex shifts through changing personal circumstances. When living with husband Mark, Lucy spent considerable time entertaining large groups of family and friends around a large multi-leaved dining table, but later wanted to disassociate herself from a distinctly "home-making" period.[8] More recently, however, she had begun to think that her small dining table might be impractical for hosting a new set of friends.

Alice is in her mid-fifties and lives in a ground-floor two-bedroom flat in an city-center townhouse. At the time of interview she did not work, having had to take early retirement on ill health grounds. Her flat was of modern design with pale kitchen cabinets and laminate flooring. Furniture discussed in the interview included several large ornate carved pieces—a sideboard, large wardrobe/cabinet, and table and chairs—of vaguely "colonial" style with wrought-iron fittings. When living in a large house in another city with her husband and daughters, Alice had enjoyed exploring antique shops, and the dark carved pieces were judged as "hers" following a divorce. In contrast to these pieces, Alice was not particularly enthusiastic about the 1960s Danish furniture which had been current at the time of her marriage:

> That wasn't my style. I sort of liked it at other people's places and I sort of looked at it, but when it came to my—to take the time for me to buy something, I didn't. We did have one piece [. . .] this long six-foot teak box with our stereo, radio and tape deck I guess in it. This massive thing was six feet long and had modern foot high legs and it was a brute to find a home for, let alone trying to move it around the room. It took up a whole wall, six feet is long, and then it was low, so we had pictures and things sitting on top of it, but that thing stayed with us for too many years and finally I was able to turf it. [. . .] Well, actually it was quite nice, it was very simple, but it was good teak and I took good care of it. It would certainly be an attractive piece for somebody who wanted that sort of thing, but I had it with me for 15 or 20 years and I was tired of it.

There are a number of important aspects to Alice's story, including the interesting shift between what "I" and "we" when referring to furniture purchased during her marriage. Alongside a general narrative of joint decision-making and collective home consumption, the story of divesting herself of a specific piece of furniture representative of a previous relationship also is prominent.

CONCLUSIONS

For Miller (1998: 141), "shopping is not about possessions per se, nor is it about identity per se. It is about obtaining goods, or imagining the possession and use of goods." Utilizing the notion of home consumption to encompass the arrangement, acquisition, disposal as well as purchase of domestic goods, we similarly have sought to emphasize the fluid and ongoing nature of consumption practices in the home. Illuminating the complexity and diversity of women's and men's engagements with homemaking helps us progress beyond a binary opposition between individual identity construction by a singular consumer and consumption which is oriented towards a family project. As Gullestad (1995: 319–20) notes: "the home is a rich, flexible and ambiguous symbol; it can simultaneously signify individual identity, family solidarity and a whole range of other values."

A key aim of this article has been to attempt to push further discussions of the relationship between ". . . people and the objects which . . . define the self" (Parr 1999a: 117). We have sought to move beyond generalized theorizations of the reflexive self in late modernity so favored by authors such as Giddens (1991, 1992) and Beck (1992) and yet at the same time to address the potentially collective nature of homemaking within shared households. With respect to Miller (1998), we would not wish to characterize individual homemaking aspirations as always and everywhere looking towards a nuclear family setting. Home consumption may not be closely equated with family formation or a shared domestic identity. As we have seen, home consumption and identity construction are connected in a range of ways and via a diversity of mechanisms. For lone householders, identity construction through home consumption can be important at certain times and places even though their domestic circumstances are not those of the traditional nuclear family. The forging of individual identity may be important as single men or women are beginning domestic life away from a parental home; or alternatively later in the life cycle following the dissolution of a shared household. For couples or shared householders, homemaking practices may at particular moments represent collective endeavors, whilst at other times one partner may invest more attention in the home project than the other. In some relationships there may be a drive toward self-expression, even at the same time that relationships themselves have become increasingly subject to dialogue and negotiation. Both the making of the landscape inside the home and the narration of this making are ongoing projects undertaken within and through the diverse webs of relationship among individuals within a household.

ACKNOWLEDGMENTS

The research upon which this article is based was funded by the Economic and Social Research Council (Award No. R000237580) and the Social Sciences and Humanities Research Council of Canada (Award No. 410-97-0335). We are grateful to Paul Stallard and Erica Spreitzer for their research assistance, and to interviewees for sharing their experiences with us. Thanks also to two anonymous referees for their most thoughtful and constructive comments and suggestions.

NOTES

1. Although the broader study from which this article derives sought to focus specifically on furniture, our conversations with consumers frequently stretched to encompass decorative objects, artwork, and electrical goods.
2. Interviewees did differ across categories such as age, marital status, and sexuality (Leslie and Reimer 2003a: 295). Both homeowners and tenants were included in the study.
3. Quotations thus do not identify the nationality of consumers. We have reflected elsewhere upon potential national differences in consumer

attitudes to and awareness of environmental issues in furniture production (Reimer and Leslie 2004).

4. Thanks to one of the article's referees for emphasizing this point.

5. All names used in this article have been changed.

6. We are extremely grateful to an anonymous referee for encouraging us to focus more carefully upon the nuances of conversations with Sarah and several other interviewees.

7. On the strong appeal of "maple as modern" to Canadian consumers, see Parr (1999b).

8. During her marriage to Mark, Lucy did also work full-time as a secretary.

REFERENCES

BBC2. 1997. *All Mod Cons*, "The DIY pioneers" (episode 1 of 3).

Bauman, Z. 1998. *Work, Consumerism and the New Poor*. Buckingham: Open University Press.

Beck, U. 1992. *Risk Society: Towards a New Modernity*. London: Sage.

Beck, U. and E. Beck-Gernsheim. 2002. *Individualization: Institutionalised Individualism and its Social and Political Consequences*. London: Sage.

Bourdieu, P. 1984. *Distinction: A Social Critique of the Judgement of Taste*. Trans. R. Nice. London: Routledge.

Carrier, J. 1995. *Gifts and Commodities: Exchange and Western Capitalism since 1700*. London: Routledge.

Chapman, T. and J. Hockey (eds). 1999. *Ideal Homes: Social Change and Domestic Life*. London: Routledge.

Cieraad, I. (ed.). 1999. *At Home: An Anthropology of Domestic Space*. Syracuse, NY: Syracuse University Press.

Clarke, A. 2001. "The Aesthetics of Social Aspiration." In D. Miller (ed.) *Home Possessions: Material Culture behind Closed Doors*, pp. 23–45. Oxford: Berg.

de Grazia, V. 1996. "Introduction." In V de Grazia with H Furlough (eds) *The Sex of Things: Gender and Consumption in Historical Perspective*. Berkeley, CA: University of California Press.

Dowling, R. and G. Pratt. 1995. "Home Truths: Recent Feminist Constructions." *Urban Geography* 14: 464–75.

Fine, B. and E. Leopold. 1993. *The World of Consumption*. London, Routledge.

Giddens, A. 1991. *Modernity and Self-Identity*. Cambridge: Polity

Giddens, A. 1992. *The Transformation of Intimacy*. Cambridge: Polity

Gronow, J. and A. Warde. 2001. "Introduction." In J. Gronow and A. Warde (eds) *Ordinary Consumption*, pp. 1–8. London: Routledge.

Gullestad, M. 1995. "Home-Decoration as Popular Culture." In S. Jackson and S. Moores (eds) *The Politics of Domestic Consumption: Critical Readings*, pp. 319–35. London: Prentice Hall.

Hunt, P. 1995. "Gender and the Construction of Home Life." In S. Jackson and S. Moores (eds) *The Politics of Domestic Consumption*, pp. 301–13. London: Prentice-Hall.

Jackson, P. and Holbrook, B. 1995. "Multiple Meanings: Shopping and the Cultural Politics of Identity." *Environment and Planning A* 27: 1913–30.

Johnson, L. 1996. "'As Housewives we are Worms': Women, Modernity and the Home Question." *Cultural Studies* 10: 449–63.

Lash, S. and Friedman, J.(eds). 1996 [1992]. *Modernity and Identity*. Oxford: Blackwell.

Leslie, D. and Reimer, S. 2003a. "Gender, Modern Design and Home Consumption." *Environment and Planning D: Society and Space* 21: 293–316.

Leslie, D. and Reimer, S. 2003b. "Fashioning Furniture: Restructuring the Furniture Commodity Chain." *Area* 35: 427–37.

Löfgren, O. 1990. "Consuming Interests." *Culture and History* 7: 7–36.

Lunt, P.K. and S. M. Livingstone. 1992. *Mass Consumption and Personal Identity: Everyday Economic Experience*. Buckingham: Open University Press.

MacDonald, S. and J. Porter. 1990. *Putting on the Style: Setting up Home in the 1950s*. London: The Geffrye Museum.

Madigan, R. and M. Munro. 1996. "'House Beautiful': Style and Consumption in the Home." *Sociology* 30: 41–57.

Madigan, R., M. Munro and S. Smith. 1990. "Gender and the Meaning of Home." *International Journal of Urban and Regional Research* 14: 625–47.

Miller, D. 1991 [1987]. *Material Culture and Mass Consumption*. Oxford: Blackwell.

Miller, D. 1998. *A Theory of Shopping*. Cambridge: Polity

Miller, D. (ed.). 2001. *Home Possessions: Material Culture behind Closed Doors*. Oxford: Berg

Miller, D., P. Jackson, N. Thrift, B. Holbrook and M. Rowlands. 1998. *Shopping, Place and Identity*. London: Routledge.

Munro, M. and R. Madigan. 1999. "Negotiating Space in the Family Home." In I. Cieraad (ed.) *At Home: An Anthropology of Domestic Space*, pp. 107–17. Syracuse: Syracuse University Press.

Parr, J. 1999a. "Household Choices as Politics and Pleasure in 1950s Canada." *International Labour and Working Class History* 55: 112–28.

Parr, J. 1999b. *Domestic Goods: The Material, the Moral and the Economic in the Postwar Years*. Toronto: University of Toronto Press.

Pratt, G. 1981. "The House as an Expression of Social Worlds." In J. Duncan (ed.) *Housing and Identity: Cross-Cultural Perspectives*, pp. 135–80. London: Croom Helm.

Pred, A. 1995. "Interfusions: Consumption, Identity and the Practices and Power Relations of Everyday Life." *Environment and Planning A* 28: 11–24.

Putnam, T. 1999. "'Postmodern' Home Life." In I. Cieraad (ed.) *At Home: An Anthropology of Domestic Space*, pp. 144–52. Syracuse: Syracuse University Press.

Putnam, T. and C. Newton (eds). 1990. *Household Choices*. London: Futures Publications.

Reimer, S. and D. Leslie. 2004. "Knowledge, Ethics and Power in the Home Furnishings Commodity Chain." In Alex Hughes and Suzanne Reimer (eds) *Geographies of Commodity Chains*, pp. 252–273. London: Routledge.

Seeley, J., A. Sim and E. W. Loosley. 1956. *Crestwood Heights: A Study of the Culture of Suburban Life*. Toronto: University of Toronto Press.

Shove, E. 1999. "Constructing Home: A Crossroads of Choices." In I. Cieraad (ed.) *At Home: An Anthropology of Domestic Space*, pp. 130–43. Syracuse, NY: Syracuse University Press.

Shove, E. and A. Warde. 2002. "Inconspicuous Consumption: The Sociology of Consumption, Lifestyles and the Environment." In R. Dunlap, F. Buttel, P. Dickens and A. Gijsnijt (eds) *Sociological Theory and the Environment*, pp. 230–51. Lanham, MD: Rowman and Littlefield.

Slater, D. 1997. *Consumer Culture and Modernity*. Cambridge: Polity.

Valentine, G. 1999. "Eating in: Home, Consumption and Identity." *The Sociological Review* 47: 491–524.

HOME CULTURES

NOTES TO CONTRIBUTORS

- Articles should be approximately 5,000 to 8,000 words (but not exceeding 8,000 words in length unless by prior agreement please).
- They must include a three-sentence biography of the author(s) and an abstract.
- Interviews should not exceed 15 pages and do not require an author biography.
- Exhibition and book reviews are normally 500 to 1,000 words in length but review articles can be between 1,000 and 2,000 words.
- The Publishers will require a disk as well as a hard copy of any contributions.

From time to time, *Home Cultures* plans to produce special issues devoted to a single topic with a guest editor. Persons wishing to organize a topical issue are invited to submit a proposal which contains a 100-word description of the topic together with a list of potential contributors and paper subjects. Proposals are accepted only after a review by the Journal editors and in-house editorial staff at Berg Publishers.

MANUSCRIPTS

- Manuscripts should be submitted to:
  Clare Melhuish, Editorial Administrator, *Home Cultures*, Department of Anthropology, University College London, Gower Street, London WC1E 6BT or to <homecultures@ucl.ac.uk>.
- Manuscripts will be acknowledged and entered into the review process discussed below.
- Manuscripts without illustrations will not be returned unless the author provides a self-addressed stamped envelope.
- Submission of a manuscript to the journal will be taken to imply that it is not being considered elsewhere, in the same form, in any language, without the consent of the editor and publisher. It is a condition of acceptance by the editor of a manuscript for publication that the publishers automatically acquire the copyright of the published article throughout the world. *Home Cultures* does not pay authors for their manuscripts nor does it provide retyping, drawing, or mounting of illustrations.

STYLE

- US spelling and mechanicals are to be used. Authors are advised to consult The Chicago Manual of Style (14th Edition) as a guideline for style. Webster's Dictionary is our arbiter of spelling. We encourage the use of major subheadings and, where appropriate, second-level subheadings.
- Manuscripts submitted for consideration as an article must contain:
  – a title page with the full title of the article, the author(s) name and address
  – a three-sentence biography for each author.
- Do not place the author's name on any other page of the manuscript.

MANUSCRIPT PREPARATION

- Manuscripts must be typed double-spaced (including quotations, notes and references cited), on one side only, with at least one-inch margins on standard paper using a typeface no smaller than 12pts.
- The original manuscript and a copy of the text on disk (please ensure it is clearly marked with the word-processing program that has been used) must be submitted, along with original photographs (to be returned).
- Authors should retain a copy for their records.
- Any necessary artwork must be submitted with the manuscript.

FOOTNOTES

- Footnotes appear as 'Notes' at the end of articles.
- Authors are advised to include footnote material in the text whenever possible.
- Notes are to be numbered consecutively throughout the paper and are to be typed double-spaced at the end of the text
- ***(Please do not use any footnoting or end-noting programs which your software may offer as this text becomes irretrievably lost at the typesetting stage.)***

REFERENCES

- The list of references should be limited to, and inclusive of, those publications actually cited in the text.
- References are to be cited in the body of the text in parentheses with author's last name, the year of original publication, and page number – e.g. (Rouch 1958: 45).
- Titles and publication information appear as 'References' at the end of the article and should be listed alphabetically by author and chronologically for each author.
- Names of journals and publications should appear in full. Film and video information appear as 'Filmography'.
- References cited should be typed double-spaced on a separate page.
- References not presented in the style required will be returned to the author for revision.

TABLES

- All tabular material should be part of a separately numbered series of 'Tables'.
- Each table must be typed on a separate sheet and identified by a short descriptive title.
- Footnotes for tables appear at the bottom of the table.
- Marginal notations on manuscripts should indicate approximately where tables are to appear.

FIGURES

All illustrative material: drawings, maps, diagrams, and photographs should be designated 'Figures'. They must be submitted in a form suitable for publication without redrawing.

- Drawings should be carefully done with India ink on either hard, white, smooth-surfaced board or good quality tracing paper. Ordinarily, computer-generated drawings are not of publishable quality.
- Color photographs are encouraged by the publishers. These will be reproduced in color in the print and on-line versions of the journal.
- Photographs should be glossy prints and should be numbered on the back to key with captions. Whenever possible, photographs should be 8 × 10 inches.
- The publisher also encourages artwork to be submitted as scanned files (300dpi or above ONLY) on disc or via email.
- All figures should be numbered consecutively.
- All captions should be typed double-spaced on a separate page.
- Marginal notations on manuscripts should indicate approximately where figures are to appear.
- While the editors and publishers will use all reasonable care in protecting all figures submitted, they cannot assume responsibility for their loss or damage. Authors are discouraged from submitting rare or non-replaceable materials. It is the author's responsibility to secure written copyright clearance on all photographs and drawings that are not in the public domain.

CRITERIA FOR EVALUATION

Home Cultures is a refereed journal. Manuscripts will be accepted only after review by both the editors and anonymous reviewers deemed competent to make professional judgments concerning the quality of the manuscript.

REPRINTS FOR AUTHORS

Twenty-five reprints of author's articles will be provided to the author free of charge. Additional reprints may be purchased upon request.